THE TASTEMAKER

TONY KING
THE TASTEMAKER

My life with the legends and geniuses of rock music

faber

First published in the UK in 2023
by Faber & Faber Limited
Bloomsbury House
74–77 Great Russell Street
London WC1B 3DA

Typeset by Faber & Faber Limited
Printed in the UK by CPI Group (UK) Ltd, Croydon CR0 4YY

A CIP record for this book
is available from the British Library

ISBN 978–0–571–37193–8

MIX
Paper | Supporting
responsible forestry
FSC® C171272

Printed and bound in the UK on FSC paper in line with our continuing
commitment to ethical business practices, sustainability and the environment.
For further information see faber.co.uk/environmental-policy

2 4 6 8 10 9 7 5 3

To all those friends I made along the way

1

'Seeing it's Thanksgiving, we thought we'd make tonight a little bit of a joyous occasion by inviting someone up with us onto stage. I'm sure he'll be no stranger to anyone in the audience . . . It's our great privilege and your great privilege to see and hear Mr John Lennon . . .'

I've heard some spine-tingling roars from concert crowds over the years and been in the thick of some extraordinary atmospheres. Those early Beatles concerts, with the teenage girls going wild to the point where you couldn't hear yourself think. The Stones at Hyde Park. Nina Simone at Annie's Room, with her staring down the diners who dared to eat while she sang. Later, I'd witness Elton John at Dodger Stadium. Mick Jagger and Tina Turner at Live Aid. The Rolling Stones in Argentina. But even among those many remarkable memories, there was something unique about the November night in 1974 when John Lennon walked onto the stage at Madison Square Garden to play with Elton.

The Garden has always been one of my favourite venues. It has amazing acoustics, with a cleverly designed concave ceiling that helps to capture the sound. This structure is suspended from above with a network of steel cables that allows everyone's view to be unobstructed. All of this means that when something magic happens, the Garden properly, literally rocks. That night, when John Lennon came on stage as I watched from the wings, even the limousines were bouncing in the car park.

John strode onto the stage with that unmistakeable swagger of his. His black and white Telecaster guitar matched his outfit. He was head to foot in black, with just a white gardenia pinned to the centre of his shirt and a sheriff's badge glinting in the spotlight. His long hair was a rich shade of brown, his sunglasses that familiar pair of small black circles. He exuded stardom, looked every inch the star.

Elton rose from his piano to greet him. His glasses were as large as John's were small. He'd been wearing a sort of two-piece jumpsuit, white and studded with sequins. By this point in the concert, the jacket had long gone and he was bare-chested, bar the sparkling pair of braces that were holding up his trousers. Elton was as big a star as you could get. *Goodbye Yellow Brick Road* had been released the year before and had dominated the radio airwaves ever since. As John passed, Elton gave a sort of half-bow, half-curtsey, patted John on the back as he walked to his microphone, then led the crowd in the continuing applause.

Maybe it was the combination of Elton being the biggest act on the planet and the rarity of seeing John on stage that made that welcome so overwhelming. John hadn't performed in public for years, and as events would transpire, he'd barely do so again. While all the other Beatles had enjoyed number ones with their solo work, John had found it harder to cut through with his material. His politics and the clashes with the American government of the time had made him a controversial figure in some parts of the media. But that night, the affection in the room, the love for him, was unmistakeable.

The applause continued. It rang round the Garden in waves, surging through the audience, giving me goosebumps. Elton glanced over to where I was standing. He was laughing, as if to say, 'This is going well, isn't it?' I had a lump in my throat and was clapping, smiling and nodding back. Elton and I both knew how much it had taken to get John up on stage. I felt an immense swell of pride as I stood there, and I still cherish the knowledge that I was involved in making what became one of the iconic moments in music in the 1970s happen.

———

The link between Elton and the Beatles went back to when I was working for George Martin's AIR Music in the second half of the 1960s, promoting the various acts he was recording with. When I first started working for AIR, there wasn't room for me in their main office in Baker Street, so they found me a space at Dick James Music (DJM, as it was known). Dick was the publisher of all the Beatles' music, so he had a close relationship with George. He was a lovely guy, friendly and kind.

On the front desk at the office was a girl called Charlotte, who when she wasn't answering calls used to make necklaces – beautiful long strings of love beads. Even now I still have some of them in a jar at home. On one occasion, Dick was having his weekly progress meeting, which I was meant to attend. But while I'd been talking on the telephone to some radio or TV producer, I'd been wearing and playing with some of Charlotte's necklaces, and they got all tangled up in the phone cord. As I put the phone down to go to the meeting, I realised I was completely entangled. I turned up at the meeting ten minutes late.

'I'm sorry I'm late,' I said to everyone, 'but my necklaces got caught up in the phone.'

Everyone fell about laughing, and that line became an office catchphrase. After that, every time I was late for anything I was asked if I'd had another necklace mishap.

It was at Dick James's office that I first met Elton – or Reg, as he was at the time. He was fantastically shy back then, wouldn't say boo to a goose. He didn't seem at all like the person who'd be charismatically wowing audiences in a few years' time; he was kitted out in a jean jacket and jeans – double-denimed, if I remember correctly. The two of us couldn't have looked more different. In his autobiography, Elton said that I could have drawn attention to myself even during a Martian invasion. I was certainly quite out there when it came to fashion: as well as my love beads, I had a thing for antique silk scarves at the time, and I often wore velvet trousers and had streaks in my hair.

I could tell as we talked that Reg was quite taken by my appearance. He was a musician looking to make it, and the fact that I was working for George Martin and had previously worked with the Rolling Stones made me someone he wanted to know better. And as I got to know Reg himself, it quickly became apparent to me how much he knew about music, which left me thinking, *This guy really knows his stuff.* We immediately developed a firm friendship, and I did what I could to put work his way, to help him get that first foot on the ladder. Reg became a regular at the office, and that's where the Beatles link began.

Fast-forward to the mid-1970s, and Elton was offering a helping hand to John Lennon. On John's 1974 album *Walls and Bridges*, Elton appeared on two tracks, playing Hammond organ and singing background vocals on 'Surprise, Surprise (Sweet Bird of Paradox)', and playing piano and singing on what would become the album's most successful single, 'Whatever Gets You Thru the Night'. The inspiration for the latter came from John channel-surfing TV late at night. He had come across a Black evangelist preacher, Reverend Ike, who had told viewers, 'Let me tell you guys, it doesn't matter, it's whatever gets you through the night.' John loved that phrase and wrote it down in one of his many notebooks.

According to some accounts, the song took its original feel from 'Rock Your Baby' by George McCrae, which was a big hit at the time. Once John and Elton had recorded their parts at Record Plant East, 'Whatever Gets You Thru the Night' morphed into this pulsating potential hit, Elton's piano and John's guitar chinking and syncing in time, the bass rippling up and down underneath, with this delicious, dirty 1970s sax threatening to burst through the speakers in between the singing. Jimmy Iovine, who engineered the sessions, later said that 'John knew what he wanted . . . he was going after a noise and he knew how to get it.' 'Whatever Gets You Thru the Night' is one of those songs that is both of its time and somehow timeless as well. The freshness and the energy of the recording is still clear today; it's three and a half minutes of *joie de vivre*.

The story often told is that Elton and John had a bet in the studio: if 'Whatever Gets You Thru the Night' got to number one in the American charts, then John would appear at Elton's Thanksgiving show at Madison Square Garden. That's not quite my recollection. For all its immediacy, the song wasn't even going to be a single originally; it was only thanks to some twisting of arms by the record company that it became the first track released from the album. As I recall, Elton just wanted John to appear at Madison Square Garden with him. I was looking after John at the time, so Elton asked me to ask him. When I spoke to John, he wasn't sure at first. At this point, he hadn't played live for a couple of years, but he came back with a condition: only if 'Whatever Gets You Thru the Night' got to number one would he join Elton on stage. I think John thought it was a safe bet that such a thing would never happen. His last single, the title track from his previous album, *Mind Games*, had only made it to number eighteen on the *Billboard* charts.

John, though, hadn't reckoned for the promotional push of having Elton on the record, and that autumn, 'Whatever Gets You Thru the Night' wended its way to the top of the *Billboard* charts. I remember ringing John to tell him the news.

'Guess what?' I told him. 'Your single is number one.'

'Oh,' John replied, immediately remembering the agreement he had with Elton. 'Does that mean I have to do Madison Square Garden?'

'Well,' I said, 'you *did* promise.'

There was a pause. It went on so long I wondered if he was still there. But then John said, 'OK. I'll do it.'

———

Eight days before the Madison Square Garden show, John and I flew to Massachusetts to watch Elton perform at Boston Garden.

'He needs to see the show,' Elton had said. 'He needs to know what he is getting himself into.'

John and I had seats that were hidden behind the stage. It was quite a performance. Elton was on fire. His set that night began with 'Funeral for a Friend' and finished up with 'The Bitch Is Back'. Halfway through he played his version of 'Lucy in the Sky with Diamonds', which had John nodding along in approval. He was blown away by what he saw and heard. I remember him turning around to me and saying, 'Oh my God, is this what music has become? That sound system is *fantastic*.' John's memory was racing back to his time with the Beatles. 'God,' he remembered, 'when we played Shea Stadium we had these tiny little amps and 56,000 people in front of us. They screamed so loud we could have sung whatever we liked. It didn't make a blind bit of difference.'

He sat back and soaked up the concert and how things had changed. Even with an audience as raucous and full-throated as Elton's, the music still held its own. It wasn't just the music either: everything about a concert was on a different scale now. Backstage, for example, Elton had a lavish set-up, complete with palm trees and all this other carry-on.

'In my day, we just had a bare dressing room,' John recalled.

When Elton came out for his encore, he was wearing a pair of tiny cut-off shorts and a bib top with a heart on it. He knew where we were sitting and turned round to us and curtsied. John roared with laughter. Whatever nerves or butterflies he had about performing melted away that evening in Boston. Now he was really up for it.

We flew from Boston back down to New York on *Starship*, Elton's private plane. It was properly luxurious, with a bar, spacious, comfy seats and a bedroom. Once, on Elton's birthday, his team had arranged for Stevie Wonder to come and sing 'Happy Birthday' to him on the plane as a surprise. Elton had been in one of his moods and, not knowing what was going on, had refused to come out of his bedroom. In the end, the publicist had had to knock on the door and explain that Stevie Wonder was stood outside, waiting for him to appear.

On that flight back to New York, John and Elton were both excited about the show. 'We'll have to rehearse,' Elton said, and we discussed which songs it would be best to play. 'Imagine' was suggested, but John said he didn't want to do just the greatest hits, and because Elton was already performing 'Lucy in the Sky with Diamonds', it made sense not to play it. John proposed 'I Saw Her Standing There'. There was something about performing a Paul McCartney number that got him going. He knew no one would expect him to do that.

Elton had a great band, and the rehearsals were good fun. Every time I dropped in, you could see how much everyone was enjoying themselves. The recorded version of 'Whatever Gets You Thru the Night' was fast, but playing it live pushed it faster still. As I listened to it echo around the rehearsal studio, I thought, *This is going to go down a storm.*

———

As the rehearsals continued, I took a call from someone I wasn't expecting to hear from.

Yoko.

She and John had separated the previous summer. Since then, John had been in a relationship with May Pang, a liaison that Yoko had had a hand in engineering. Although John's appearance at Madison Square Garden was meant to be a tightly guarded secret, Yoko had found out about it, and now she wanted to come along.

'Sure,' I said, feeling less sure about how John might react to her being there.

'I don't want him to know that I am there,' Yoko continued. 'Do you think you could arrange for some seats where he won't see me?'

That seemed a better plan. 'Let me talk to Elton,' I said.

Elton, like me, was worried about John finding out. With the rehearsals going so well, he didn't want anything to give John pause about playing. We found some seats that had a good view, but which were far enough away for John not to see her. They were for Yoko and a gallery owner called Gary Lejeskey. He wasn't a date, more just someone interesting to accompany her. I was curious about why Yoko wanted to come but buried myself in the arrangements, rather than thinking too hard about it.

On the day of the performance, a package arrived backstage. Inside were two gardenias in a dish: one for Elton and one for John. They were beautiful – elegant and white, with a distinctive sweet smell.

John saw the flowers and said, 'Look at these.'

'Yes,' Elton replied. 'Yoko sent them.'

I was hyper-alert at this point. But John just stared at the flowers. Then he nodded, saying, 'Yoko loves gardenias.' Next he looked up at me, and then at Elton. 'You know, I couldn't do this show if I knew she was here.'

I remember Elton looking at me, his eyes widening in horror. Neither of us dared say anything.

'I know,' I said, breaking the silence. 'Why don't you both wear the gardenias as a way to say thank you? That would be a nice gesture.'

'Sure,' Elton said. 'Let's do that.'

We pinned the gardenias to their outfits. I'm not sure what happened to Elton's. Such was the energy of his performance that I'm not sure it would have lasted long before falling off. But John's took pride of place on his shirt and remained firmly there when he took to the stage. I knew that Yoko would see it. And I wondered what might happen next.

———

John's three-song set came halfway through Elton's show. 'Whatever Gets You Thru the Night' was played at breakneck speed, the adrenaline of the performance powering everyone through it. It was one of those moments when I could feel the crowd feeding off the energy of the band, and the band feeding off the energy of the crowd. 'Lucy in the Sky with Diamonds' I

9

knew as a regular part of Elton's set; his version started simply and slowly, before building up to a sweeping crescendo. I'm not sure John had ever sung that song live before, so hearing him and Elton combine for the chorus was awesome.

Then the time machine took everyone back further still. John introduced the final song as being by 'an old fiancé of mine named Paul. I've never sung it before.' The guitars kicked in, and the band ripped through 'I Saw Her Standing There'. That took me back a decade or so. Whatever he had back then, John still had it now. Elton's band was as tight as could be. It was slick, together, and by the time the song reached its climax, the audience were up on their feet again. John took the applause and bounced back off stage. He was buzzing, and Elton's grin was as wide as could be. We'd done it.

When the encores took place, John returned for the closing number, 'The Bitch Is Back', shaking a tambourine with the backing singers. He was having a ball.

Later, backstage, Yoko suddenly appeared.

'Oh,' John said, 'you were here.'

I don't know if he knew or suspected. Before John could begin grilling me about what I did or didn't know, I tactfully gave them some space to speak. There's a famous shot of the two of them talking that night, in which the photographer manages to capture a look passing between them. When I saw them together, you could sense the spark. The connection was undeniable.

This wasn't the moment when they got back together. That rapprochement didn't happen for some months. When we all moved off to a hotel for the afterparty, John sat with May, and Yoko sat with Gary on a separate table. There was no edge or tension there. Uri Geller, I remember, was doing the rounds, making everyone laugh with his spoon-bending. It was all very jovial and relaxed.

But I knew what I'd seen with my own eyes backstage, and what the photographer had also caught on film. *It might not be tonight, but at some point*, I thought, *something will happen.* When the pull between two people is that strong, it's hard for them to turn away.

Sitting watching Geller bending spoons in front of me was a surreal end to an amazing evening. I knew that I'd been part of something special, and for all the stimulants that 1970s rock and roll had to offer, the kick from this felt even better.

2

The first time I heard Elvis Presley, I was fourteen years old. I was having a strip wash in the kitchen one evening, listening to Radio Luxembourg, when a song came over the airwaves like nothing I'd heard before.

Growing up in Eastbourne, on the south coast of England, in the 1950s, the radio had always been something of a lifeline. I loved pop music from an early age: 'Memories Are Made of This' by Dean Martin, 'Come on-a My House' by Rosemary Clooney, 'Jezebel' by Frankie Laine, 'Old Cape Cod' by Patti Page. Ruby Murray, Eve Boswell . . . I'd got to know a galaxy of stars. I'd listen to the BBC Light Programme and then to Radio Luxembourg. It wasn't just music either: the comedy of *The Goon Show* and the science fiction of *Journey into Space* were also firm favourites. At school the next day we'd talk excitedly about what we'd heard on the radio, in the same way that future generations would talk about what they'd seen on TV.

The first time I got a hint of what rock and roll might be about was when I heard 'Flamingo' by Earl Bostic. 'Flamingo' is a fat, sexy saxophone instrumental that seems to sashay its way out of the speakers. The pop stars of the early 1950s I'd listened to had that sparkle and glamour, but Earl Bostic had a bit more swing and sway to him. There was something in the tone of his saxophone-playing that was a bit deeper, dirtier, earthier. 'Flamingo', though, turned out to be just the palate cleanser for me. 'Heartbreak Hotel' was the main course, although I didn't know who was singing it yet.

From the opening line I was sucked in. There was no backing, just this strange, vibrato singing style, punctuated by a double stab of guitar and piano. Then, as the title, 'Heartbreak Hotel', was sung, a walking bass wandered in, joining the singing for the chorus. As the next verse started up, the voice became more pronounced. The singer sang with a 'huh' and a sigh, the word 'baby' becoming 'buh-haybee'.

I ran across from the kitchen sink, where I'd been washing, skidding and slipping on the wet floor as I made for the parlour and the radio. I was dripping water everywhere. In retrospect, reaching for the radio dial with wet hands might not have been a good idea, but the only shock I got was from the music I was hearing. The radio was hissing and crackling, so I frantically turned the dial, desperate to tune in and hear the song more clearly. But almost as soon as the record had started, it had finished. The next song came on, and it was back to the usual big, glossy pop sound.

What was it I'd just heard? The space in the record. The phrasing of the singing. That voice. The hustle and shuffle and swagger of the song were intoxicating. Standing there in my kitchen in Eastbourne in 1956, water pooling by my feet, the sound felt alien, otherworldly. Even the singer's name, which I'd only just picked up, sounded strange. Elvish? Elfish? The static on the radio didn't help, and the name didn't stick in my mind.

The following morning, I was surprised by the strength of my reaction: I was frightened, terrified I might never hear the song again. It was like a key to a different way of life, and somehow I'd let it slip through my fingers. I realised that the record had had such an impact on me that I had to discover who'd sung it.

I remember going to school and meeting up with my friends in the bike sheds. They were going on about *The Goon Show*, and all I wanted to discuss was this song on the radio. But no one else had heard it or knew what I was going on about. I was desperate, this glimmer of a different existence seemingly gone for ever.

Then, a few days later, I picked up a copy of the *Daily Mirror*. I was flicking through, and there, on one of the inside pages, was a short column called 'Out of the Groove'. Among the titbits about Norrie Paramour, Billy Eckstine and Billy Daniels was the following paragraph:

> Elvis Presley, America's biggest disc-threat since Johnny Ray, has been awarded a gold record for the millionth sale of 'Heartbreak Hotel', which hasn't rocketed away in Britain yet . . .

Buh-haybee. That was him.

'Heartbreak Hotel' was Elvis's first single in the UK, and from mid-May it rose steadily up the charts, peaking at number two, where it was kept off the top spot, incongruously, by Pat Boone's 'I'll Be Home'. 'Heartbreak Hotel' would stay in the top ten for the entire summer, joined for several weeks by 'Blue Suede Shoes'.

It's difficult now to describe just what an effect that first Elvis song had on everyone who heard it. But for anyone who ended up being involved in music in the 1960s and '70s, it was instrumental. In David Kynaston's *Family Britain*, he quotes John Peel's reaction to first hearing it as similar to seeing 'a naked extra-terrestrial walking through the door and announcing that he/she was going to live with me for the rest of my life'. John Lennon's aunt Mimi remembered of her nephew that 'it was nothing but Elvis Presley, Elvis Presley, Elvis Presley'. In his memoir, Elton John remembers that the first time he saw a picture of Elvis, he was 'the most bizarre-looking man I'd ever seen'. And when he first heard 'Heartbreak Hotel', 'You could literally *feel* this strange energy he was giving off, like it was contagious.'

I didn't have a record player at that point. And I didn't have the money to buy one either. So I took on a paper round to save up, and my dad said he would pay for the hire purchase of a unit. He was a trained carpenter–joiner, so he built a cabinet for me. I started buying 78s. I became a regular fixture at the local record stores, dressing up like Elvis. I was obsessed with him and with rock and roll. I never looked back.

———

I was born in the west London suburb of Hillingdon during the war and lived in West Drayton and Yiewsley, before moving to Eastbourne, which was where I spent most of my childhood. My earliest memories are fleeting but vivid. I can still recall standing up in my cot, holding on to the railings and looking out of the window of my bedroom. The war inevitably impinged on us. There was a deadly bomb called the Doodlebug, which would drop out of the sky in silence, taking out a house almost at random. I remember a family we knew called the Warrens, who were killed in this way. They had a son whom everyone called Sonny Boy Warren. Maybe it was its weirdness that made it stick in my mind, but despite being incredibly young at the time, I can still clearly remember the word 'Doodlebug'.

I have strange memories of that first house in the suburbs of London. That was because my family situation was complicated, and it wasn't until I was ten or eleven that I understood and unravelled what was really going on. That was when I learned that the couple who were bringing me up, whom I called Mum and Dad, were actually my grandparents. My biological mother was someone I knew as Aunty Kay, while my real father, Hughie Frank, was nowhere to be seen.

Kay was the product of a backstage relationship that my grandmother (Mum) had with an actor before she met my grandfather (Dad). To complicate things further, Mum and Dad weren't married – or, rather, they were, but to different people. My dad's first wife wouldn't give him a divorce, and the same went for my mum's husband, I believe. So they lived together as common-law husband and wife, under the assumed name of Jones.

Kay worked at a munitions factory during the war. She loved to party; I inherited that off her. I remember her once telling me how she would go to 'blackout dances'. The wartime dances were always the most fun, she explained, because of the risk. Your life was in danger, and somehow that made the fun even more thrilling. I have a photo of one of those dances, with my real mother and father in it separately, before they were together. It was at another blackout dance that they met properly.

Kay ran away to get married to my real father, but pretty soon the marriage broke down. He went off with someone else, and Kay ended up with a different partner, who became the father of my half-brother, Peter. My brother's father was a bit of a rough diamond. He earned his money trading watches and other goods on the black market, and had a streak of violence in him that came out when he'd had a drink or two. My mother would be on the receiving end.

My grandparents didn't like the idea of me being brought up by someone who wasn't my father. The fact that Kay was working at the munitions factory also meant she didn't have time to be a mother to me. And so it was agreed that my grandparents would become Mum and Dad. I lived with them and Kay's sisters, Aunty Gladys and Aunty Joan. Kay became Aunty Kay, and my brother Peter I knew as my cousin. Which all sounds very confusing, but it made sense to me at the time. Aunty Kay and Peter would come and visit us. Peter and I were always very close and continually got into all sorts of scrapes and mischief. We were like brothers – and, secretly, we actually were.

When I was around eleven years old, secrets started to reveal themselves. One time, I was looking through the laundry basket when I found a photograph of a boy hidden between the sheets. It was a black-and-white photo, taken on a beach. The boy was young and had a cheeky look on his face. I later learned that this was a son from my (grand)father's first marriage. The boy had died from meningitis when he was just seven years old. One of the reasons that my grandparents had agreed to look after me was as a sort of replacement for the boy my (grand)father had lost.

While I was still trying to make sense of that, I overheard a conversation between the person whom I thought was my mother and her sister Daisy. I can't remember the reason why, whether it was a game or something, but I was hiding behind a chair. When they came in to sit down, they didn't realise I was crouching there. I stayed there, hunched up, and listened.

'So,' Daisy said, 'when are you going to tell Tony that Kay is his mother?'

'We're not,' my mum replied. 'We don't see any reason to tell him.'

I sat there, frozen and rigid. I stayed even after they'd got up and left, my mind trying to process what I'd just heard. My head was spinning. The conversation sounded crazy, but at the same time it made a strange sort of sense to me. It would help explain why my two sisters were so much older than me. I remembered, too, the confusion at school over my name: was I Tony Jones, which was my mum and dad's chosen surname, or Tony King, that of my real parents? Once, the headmaster had asked me what the true story was, and I went home and asked my father. He said, 'Tell them to mind their own business.'

Now, though, my family situation went from fogginess into focus. At the same time, it opened up more questions: if Aunty Kay was my biological mother, then who was my real father? There was no one in the family set-up who fitted the bill. That left me curious and intrigued. I didn't mention anything about the conversation I'd overheard to my parents, and nobody said anything to me. We carried on as before. I loved 'Mum and Dad' and didn't want to change that. But the next time I saw Peter, I asked him about it.

'Do you realise that we are brothers?' I asked.

Peter gave me this look, and I realised that he already knew. He'd been ordered not to say anything. Peter was the only person I spoke to about it. I think he might have told my real mother that I knew, but still nobody said anything. I learned from Peter, I think, that my real father had died. He had been killed in the war – a war hero. I was sad not to have known him, but felt proud of what he had achieved.

All of this was a big secret, and it rested heavily on my young shoulders, staying there, pressing down throughout my school years. It was only after I'd left school that I found out a little bit more. I was seventeen, and I was having a conversation with Aunty Joan about my biological father. When I mentioned that he was a war hero, she pulled a face.

'What are you saying, Joan?' I asked. 'That he wasn't a hero?' And then I worked it out. 'He didn't die?'

'Oh no,' Joan said. 'He is still around somewhere.'

And I said, 'Oh.'

After the conversation with Joan, I finally spoke to Dad about the situation. I'd come to terms with Aunty Kay being my biological mother and my real father no longer being around. But now I knew he was alive, that churned everything up all over again.

'Dad,' I asked him, 'were you ever going to tell me about Kay being my mother?'

He looked taken aback by the question. To be fair, it must have felt as though it came a little bit out of nowhere. But he gathered himself and replied, simply, 'We didn't see the need.'

I remember we both sat there in silence, deep in our different thoughts. Then Dad said, 'We have done the best we can for you.' And that was the end of the conversation.

Looking back, I wonder whether he thought I was being critical of him, or that somehow they'd let me down. I wasn't, and they hadn't. I knew he and Mum had always been there for me, and always would be. And I loved them equally in return. It might have been a complicated beginning, but the feelings I had for my parents were simple and straightforward. The time to look for my actual father, I realised, wasn't now. I knew at some point I was going to have to see if I could find my real father, but I also realised it wasn't going to be for a long time, because I didn't want to upset my parents. In fact, it wouldn't be for decades, until after their deaths.

———

When I was a few years old, Mum became unwell. She was coughing and wheezing, and when she went to see the doctor about it, she was diagnosed with tuberculosis and sent to hospital. When she came home, I was pleased to see her, but even at my young age could sense that she still wasn't right. She had lost weight and wasn't herself. Dad decided she would benefit from getting away from the outskirts of London, and so we packed up and left, leaving West Drayton behind for a new life in the south coast resort of Eastbourne.

Mum needed fresh air to help her recovery, and compared to the capital Eastbourne had it by the bucketload. There was an open-air hospital nestled in the South Downs, just above the town, and when we first moved south, Mum stayed there to aid her recovery. As part of the fresh-air routine, the patients slept with the doors open, and Mum would tell me about how foxes would come in from the Downs at night. Once she woke up to find a fox scrabbling around under her bed. As she came to and stirred, it bolted for the open door, a flash of russet in the moonlight. But the open air of the hospital helped her make a full recovery. The weight that she'd lost was put back on – so much so that when she was discharged and returned home, I was almost embarrassed about how heavy she now was.

We lived on a street called The Circus. It was at the top of a hill and had got its name because the street was completely circular. There was a large house in the middle called The Mount and a curved row of houses on either side. We lived in number 10. Because Mum was still in hospital, Dad took me down to the local school, St Andrew's, to enrol. I liked the place and quickly made friends. I was a bright kid and did well in lessons, and when it came time to take the eleven-plus exam, I passed. In fact, I was top boy and was presented with the *Oxford Pocket Dictionary* as a prize. I've still got it: it has 'Top Boy' inscribed inside it.

Those early childhood years were idyllic. Eastbourne had the sea, the open countryside of the Downs and plenty of places for young children to explore. Nearby, along the coast, were Beachy Head, Birling Gap and Pevensey Bay. There was a castle at Pevensey Bay where Winston Churchill spent time during the war. All around us were nature and history to explore and fire our young imaginations.

It turned out it wasn't just Mum who benefited from the fresh air; I must have spent most of those early-childhood summers outdoors, leaving me permanently suntanned, as brown as a berry.

In the late 1940s and early '50s, the scars of war were still in evidence in Eastbourne. It hadn't been as badly affected as London, but you didn't need to go far to see signs of what had happened. The Marks & Spencer department store had been blown up, and dotted around the town and countryside were other landmarks that had been hit. There was an area of beach just outside Eastbourne called The Crumbles and a place called Martello Towers, which had been used as a lookout. The beach had been mined, and although they tried to clear it after the war, they'd still find mines every now and again. Others would wash up onto the beach, their spikes sticking out of the water. They'd be dealt with by the army, and the noise of exploding mortars in the background became so normal growing up, you didn't think twice about it.

Back in the house, too, the signs of war lingered. Our gas masks were still stored in a cupboard under the stairs; those were kept for a long time. My dad had made wartime toys, and I kept those too. We had ration books after the war like everybody else, but I was too young to know any different about shortages and thought that that was just how it was. Looking back, money was tight. We couldn't really afford to buy lots of new things, and if clothes got worn out, they were patched up rather than replaced. All my trousers and jackets were like that. But at the time, that was just how things were, that wartime mentality of making do and mending lingering on.

As a young child, bombsites were simply another place where we could play and explore. Strange as it may seem now, those were our playgrounds. One game we'd play would be to hide behind the mounds that the bombs had made and try and land different objects in a can – cabbages, carrots, anything we could get hold of. Nature also played its part: a group of us would go out and do dreadful things like bird-nesting – hunting for eggs and birds that were nesting. On other occasions, we'd go fishing for tadpoles, returning triumphantly with our finds and depositing them in a bath of water in the back garden to watch them grow. Bicycle rides were another big part of growing up. Before I went to grammar school, my parents bought me a Raleigh bike. This seemed like a luxury of luxuries, and knowing how tight we were for money, it meant all the more to me. Mum would make me sandwiches, and I'd go off for the day, cycling twenty miles along the coast to Hastings and back. The sandwiches never lasted long: I'd stop and eat them before halfway.

———

I was good-looking as a boy; handsome, if it is OK to say that. I knew I must have been attractive because I had a number of female friends who wanted to hang out with me. But I was all about the boys.

I was nine or ten years old when I first realised I was gay. From an early age, I knew it was in me, was part of me. It never felt like a decision or choice I had made. I never had a crossroads moment when I decided to turn left rather than right or anything like that. It was just who I was.

I had this recurring daydream that a man would come along and rescue me. To begin with, these fantasies were all about people in uniforms: firemen and those in similar professions became my heroes, and I'd dream about them. There's a Coldplay song called 'Fix You', and as a teenager I wanted what Chris Martin would later sing about: I wanted to be fixed by somebody. I wanted someone to come along and take care of me and make things right. As I grew older, there was a sexual element, too, but it was the fixing element that I found myself focusing on. That is why when I did eventually fall in love with someone, I fell for them hard.

Back in my early teens, I didn't really understand what being gay meant and didn't have the language to articulate it. It was only when I came across the word 'homosexual' in a book at school that things started to fall into place. I remember going to the school library to find a dictionary and looking up what it meant. 'Persons attracted to members of the same sex,' I read. A penny dropped. *I guess that's what I am then*, I thought. I didn't mention what I had discovered to anyone else, but I felt relief at finally being able to understand what my feelings were about.

The library became something of a sanctuary and a place of understanding. I can't remember how, but I came across the playwright Tennessee Williams. I started taking his plays out of the library, and reading through them things clicked further into place. When I was older, I went to see all the films made of the plays – *Cat on a Hot Tin Roof, The Fugitive Kind, Suddenly Last Summer* – and fell in love with them all over again. I instinctively understood the homosexual content of the writing, and I wasn't the only one. There's a famous television interview that Williams went on to give to David Frost. 'I think that everybody has some elements of homosexuality in him,' Williams told Frost, 'even the most heterosexual of us.' Frost replied, 'That no one is all man or all woman, you mean?' Williams's response was, 'In my experience, no. I don't want to be part of some sort of scandal, but I've covered the waterfront.' The applause and laughter from the audience marked one of those moments when you realise that people are often ahead of where you think they are. And actually, most people are more comfortable with the truth than you might expect.

I never got the chance to meet and talk to Tennessee Williams, but I'll never forget the occasion when I saw him in New York. It was when I was living there in the 1970s, and I was walking down Fifth Avenue, heading past St Patrick's Cathedral. In the opposite direction coming towards me, arm in arm, were three instantly identifiable figures: Truman Capote, Andy Warhol and Tennessee Williams. Williams was wearing a beautiful thick fur coat, and the three of them were laughing and in high spirits. I guess they were on their way back from a jolly lunch or some such. This was years before mobile phones, of course; if it had been now, I'd have caught the moment on camera. As it is, I just have that fleeting flash of memory to remind me of the day I saw my teenage inspiration.

Williams wasn't the only author I connected with. The novel *The City and the Pillar* by Gore Vidal told the story of a young man discovering his homosexuality. *City of Night*, John Rechy's book about hustling in Hollywood, was also important. I remember, too, devouring *Giovanni's Room* by James Baldwin when it came out. That was a big deal at the time: one of the first great openly gay novels, it tells the story of an American living in Paris, and particularly his relationship with an Italian bartender called Giovanni. Baldwin wrote beautifully and thoughtfully. His characters felt real, and I, like many readers, responded to that.

Compared to the flowing descriptions of gay life in Paris and Hollywood I'd been reading about, the reality of 1950s Eastbourne was somewhat more prosaic, and in fact as a teenager it was almost impossible to find any evidence of the existence of gay life at all. Its secrecy was not without good reason. Homosexuality in the 1950s was not only illegal in Britain, but those involved were actively pursued by the police for prosecution. Maxwell Fyfe, the Home Secretary, told parliament in 1953 that 'Homosexuals, in general, are exhibitionists and proselytisers and a danger to others, especially the young. So long as I hold the office of Home Secretary I shall give no countenance to the view that they should not be prevented from being such a danger.' Sir Lawrence Dunn, Chief Metropolitan Magistrate, described homosexuals as 'the lowest of the low'.

In 1954, there were over a thousand men in prison for homosexual acts. I'd read newspaper reports or catch snippets on the radio news about high-profile men charged with homosexual offences, John Gielgud, Rupert Croft-Cooke, Lord Montagu of Beaulieu, Peter Wildeblood and Alan Turing among them. This led to the 1957 Wolfenden Report, a government inquiry led by Sir John Wolfenden into 'Homosexual Offences and Prostitution'. During the discussions around the report, homosexuals and prostitutes were nicknamed 'Huntley and Palmers', supposedly to protect the ears of the women present. Such was the atmosphere at the time, the gay men who agreed to give evidence to the committee did so under pseudonyms such as 'the Doctor' and 'Mr White' to protect their identities.

The report's conclusions were important, claiming that 'It is not, in our view, the function of the law to intervene in the private life of citizens, or to seek to enforce any particular pattern of behaviour.' It concluded that there 'must remain a realm of private morality and immorality which is, in brief and crude terms, not the law's business' and recommended that homosexual acts between two consenting adults should no longer be a criminal offence. Wise words, but it would be another decade before this recommendation became law.

So back in Eastbourne, as a gay teenager, it made sense to keep my sexuality a secret. I certainly didn't tell my friends at school. I didn't discuss it with my family, with the exception of Aunty

Gladys, whom I'd always liked and trusted. When I was sixteen, I told her I thought I might be gay. Her response was simply that 'We all have our crosses to bear.' After that, I didn't mention it to anyone else.

Instead, and in the years that followed, my family and I skirted around the issue, without ever mentioning it directly. Later, my real mother told me that she had found a gay pub that she liked going to, which I think was her way of messaging that she was OK with it. On another occasion in the 1980s, after I had moved to America, I was back in Britain staying with my mum when I saw that a TV programme about Christopher Isherwood was on. The year before, when I was living in California, I'd been fortunate enough to meet Isherwood at a fancy-dress party in West Hollywood, where he was dressed up as an admiral of the fleet (an idea I stole for Elton's sixtieth-birthday bash, but that is another story). Isherwood was beautiful, an older man with the most exquisite eyes. The programme was on late at night on BBC2, and I said to Mum that I was going to watch it, and that it was probably too late for her. To my surprise, Mum said that she'd stay up and watch it with me. In the programme, Isherwood was very explicit about his sexuality: he talked about how he lived with Don Bachardy, about David Hockney . . . all sorts. I was watching it with half an eye on Mum, thinking, *I wonder what she is making of all of this.*

At the end of the programme, I got up to switch the television off.

'Oh, what a shame that had to finish,' Mum said. 'I could easily have listened to another half-hour of him. What an interesting man.'

The following day, I had lunch with my real mother, who was living round the corner at the time.

'I saw this programme last night,' she said, 'about this most interesting man.'

'You mean Christopher Isherwood?' I asked.

'Yes, that was him.'

'We watched it, too,' I said. 'Mum said she could have done another half-hour.'

'Oh, I really loved it,' my real mother said. 'I feel the same way.'

Both of them, I think, saw past his sexuality to what he was like as a human being. Isherwood's homosexuality was part and parcel of who he was, but it wasn't the biggest deal. The big deal was that this was a very interesting man who talked about life in a very interesting way. After that, Isherwood became my role model. *I don't mind being known as a gay man*, I decided, *but I would really like to be known as an interesting man.*

Perhaps both my mother and real mother were trying to tell me something too. Neither of them felt able to talk about my sexuality directly, but by talking about Christopher Isherwood they could do so at one remove, and this was their way of acknowledging it. Because they liked Isherwood, it didn't just mean that they were OK with him being gay, and, hence, me being gay by proxy; it meant, too, that they were much more interested in him as a human being. And in our strange family swirl of secrets and things left unsaid, I like to think that they were trying to tell me that they thought of me in that same way.

3

'King!' The headmaster's voice boomed across the classroom. 'King, where are you?'

The entire class turned round to look in my direction. I shrank in my seat, a little unnerved as to why the headmaster, Mr Shaw, had burst into our lesson, unannounced, and why I'd been singled out. Mr Shaw, known to everyone as Toady, was someone I'd never particularly liked, and as I raised my hand, he stared down at me with contempt. Whatever the reason why Mr Shaw had called me out, it seemed unlikely that it had to do with praise.

As much as I'd loved my time at junior school, I hated grammar school. Hated it. I didn't like the atmosphere: I found it oppressive and bullying. The pressure to do well bore down on me the whole time: if you didn't deliver results, you were left to feel bad about yourself. I used to dread exam week in particular. I'd get really nervous and upset in advance. Dad always tried to encourage me: 'Just do the best that you can,' he'd tell me. But however hard I tried, I couldn't escape the sense that my best was never going to be quite good enough.

I knew I was unhappy at the school. I told my parents and asked if I could leave and go somewhere else. But for some reason I never did. I just stayed on and continued to suffer. And once I heard 'Heartbreak Hotel', any thoughts of working hard to get into university went out of the window. I just wanted to get myself out of there as quickly as possible.

Throughout my time at grammar school, there were only two teachers whom I really liked, and who seemed to like me back. One was my history teacher, Roy Hilton. When he left, I organised a whip-round for him, and with the money I collected I bought a Goons 78: 'I'm Walking Backwards for Christmas'. When I gave it to him, I could see he was genuinely touched that I had made this effort to say thank you and goodbye.

The other teacher I liked was my art teacher, whom everyone called Romeo. From an early age I had been fascinated by art and drawing, and he responded to my interest. He knew that I liked to paint and draw, and rather than pressuring me like all the other teachers, he encouraged me to be creative and think differently. Once, he gave us the task of coming up with a book cover that represented a county of England. I chose Cornwall, and decided to illustrate it with one of those false lights that were once used by wreckers to lure ships onto the rocks. I remember him telling me how impressed he was, and how he appreciated that I'd done something different.

'Heartbreak Hotel' was the wrecking lamp of my school career. Once I'd heard that song, and the siren voice of Elvis Presley, there was no going back. I felt different to the other boys. I changed how I dressed, trying to copy Elvis. And I fell in love, properly in love, with music. Getting that first record player was just the start. Now I wanted to hear and play every new tune I could get my hands on.

I started to hang out in the various record shops in Eastbourne. I'd go in and ask them if they had the new Elvis Presley record in, buying 'Hound Dog', 'All Shook Up' and 'Too Much'. I also bought records by other singers that I liked: Tommy Steele, Guy Mitchell, Johnny Ray. And even when I wasn't buying music, I liked to hang around the stores anyway. There was something exciting about the racks of records and the music being played over the shop's speakers. The other people loitering in there felt like kindred spirits. These were the days before listening booths; all the records were behind the counter, so you had to go up and ask for whichever one you wanted.

One of the shops I used to hang out in was called the Golden Record Salon. It was owned by a guy called Bill Sapsford. As well as running the shop, Bill also worked in London for Decca Records – not just a record company but perhaps THE record company at the time. To an Eastbourne boy, that seemed ridiculously glamorous. He and his wife seemed to like me, and I started to help out: first I used to clean his car for him, before graduating to a Saturday job working in the record store itself.

As much as I hated school, I loved working in that shop. It felt like a dream job – I got to listen to and play music all day long. People would come in asking for records, and I'd find them among the racks of 78s and 45s. If they wanted to hear the song first, then I'd play it for them over the store's loudspeakers. If it was good, then by the time the record finished, other customers would be asking for a copy as well.

At school I always felt I was treated as though I knew nothing, but in the record store people took me seriously. I began to develop a knowledge of music, and people would ask me for recommendations. I also began to make suggestions to Bill as to which records he should stock. 'A Whole Lotta Shakin' Going On' by Jerry Lee Lewis was one I told him to get in, and it shifted by the bucketload. Not all my suggestions were as successful, mind. 'Short Fat Fannie' by Larry Williams was a less hot tip of mine, our copies lying there gathering dust (I still think it's a great record, though).

Fortunately, it was Jerry Lee Lewis rather than 'Short Fat Fannie' that stuck in Bill's mind, and one day he said there was a job going at the record label and asked me whether I'd be interested. For a teenage boy who hated school and loved music, the offer felt like a golden ticket. The problem was my age. I was still only fifteen and had my GCEs coming up, which I was dreading. I asked my parents if I could leave school before the exams. They were quite taken aback at first. They loved me and wanted me to be happy, but to leave school without any qualifications was something of a gamble, not least because the music business was still something of an unknown quantity. Was rock and roll here to stay, or was it, as some naysayers suggested, more of a passing fad? I was desperate for the opportunity, so I took Bill to meet my parents and help me make my case. And, to their eternal credit, they agreed to let me go.

However, this was why the headmaster, Toady, was bursting into my lesson and singling me out. My delight in leaving was matched by his fury about me going. Boys didn't leave grammar school before their exams. It just wasn't done. Toady was determined to make an example of me. He felt I needed bringing to heel and to be made an example of, perhaps to deter any others with similar plans in mind. And so he tore a strip off me, told everyone how stupid I was being, throwing my education away for a job in an industry that probably wouldn't even be around in a couple of years. Toady, unsurprisingly, was one of those people who didn't get Elvis. I felt humiliated in front of everyone, but rather than making me change my mind, it just further strengthened my resolve.

Later, he collared me in the corridor, a triumphant look on his face. 'You can't leave,' he told me. 'You're not allowed to leave school until your sixteenth birthday. Correct me if I'm wrong, but you're only fifteen.'

I tried to stop the smile from spreading too far across my face. 'I am sixteen on Friday,' I replied. And on that Friday, 14 March

1958, I left school. I had the weekend off, then started in the music business on the Monday. On the day I left, I cycled home, bursting with a sense of freedom. School was over. I went into the garden and set fire to my school cap, watching as the flames flickered and the smoke spiralled into the sky.

Many, many years later, I bumped into my old headmaster again. I'd been in the States and was coming back to Eastbourne to see my mum. I'd flown in on Concorde, then caught the train down to the coast. There in the carriage, sitting diagonally opposite me with a group of people, was Toady. No future, he'd told me. Throwing my life away, he'd sneered. Here I was, fresh off Concorde. I was so tempted to say something, but instead I sat back in my seat. I didn't need to justify myself to anybody. I was leading the life I wanted to live.

———

On 17 March – St Patrick's Day – 1958, I caught the 7.12 a.m. train from Eastbourne to London. I was both nervous and excited as I watched the countryside rumble past through the carriage window. London was still a long way from swinging in the late 1950s, and around me sat suited men, all briefcases and umbrellas. Arriving in the capital, I made my way down Vauxhall Bridge Road. Everything felt bustling and exciting: the red buses and black taxis, the people. Suddenly, my regular short bike ride to school felt parochial in the extreme. Compared to Eastbourne, London felt *alive*. I crossed the Thames, heading for the Albert Embankment. On either side of me, I watched the sweep and curve of the river. Landmarks leaped out: the Houses of Parliament on one side, the recently built Royal Festival Hall and South Bank on the other.

At number 9, Albert Embankment, I saw the gleam of a company sign by the door: Decca Records. My throat felt dry, but I took a deep breath and marched in. My life in the music business was about to begin.

Decca was one of the biggest names in the record industry. Originally formed back in 1929, it found early success in the pre-war years with artists such as Al Jolson, Cab Calloway and George Formby. By 1939, it was selling over a third of all the records bought in the US. By the 1950s, Decca's roster included labels such as London, Brunswick, RCA and Coral. They hit big early on in the rock and roll era by signing Bill Haley and the Comets, whose 'Rock Around the Clock' became a worldwide smash in 1954. And via their London American label, they were able to license acts from US independents such as Chess, Sun and Tamla.

My first job was as assistant progress chaser. I worked in the sleeves department, and it was my role to help make sure the covers were properly put together. In those days, record covers would all have sleeve notes. Someone would be tasked with writing these, and as my job title suggests, I had to chase their progress and get them approved by the relevant label boss. I'd do the same with the artwork proofs – get them checked, signed off and ready to go to the printers.

As jobs went, it was a great way into the industry. I was immediately in touch with a lot of people around the building, which in turn meant that everyone knew who I was. I probably stood out anyway: I was very young, only just sixteen, wasn't bad-looking and was incredibly talkative. My passion for music, and for rock and roll in particular, must have poured off me. My delight at being there was clear for all to see, as was my enthusiasm for the job. Within six months I had been offered three other positions in the company.

One of the people who approached me was Geoff Milne, who was the label manager for London American Records. He asked me if I'd like to work for him as assistant label manager. It sounded like my dream job. Here I was, having drenched myself in 1950s Americana back in Eastbourne, and now I was being offered the chance to work on this incredible selection of American artists: Little Richard, Fats Domino, Jerry Lee Lewis, the Drifters, the Ronettes, the Crystals . . . the list just went on and on. The other jobs I'd been offered were exciting in their own ways as well, but how could I say no to this opportunity?

Geoff trusted my enthusiasm and taste in music. He gave me the task of compiling EPs. I'd select the four tracks, come up with a cover and see the whole thing through to production. Because I had an ear for a song, my selections were good, and the EPs would sell well. I did one for the Everly Brothers. For Little Richard I chose songs including 'The Girl Can't Help It', 'Lucille', 'Long Tall Sally' and 'Tutti Frutti'. For Fats Domino I plucked out numbers like 'I'm in Love Again', 'Blueberry Hill' and 'Walking to New Orleans'. Each of my EPs would have four big hits squeezed onto it, packaged within a nice, glossy, laminated cover.

Looking back, being assistant label manager at such a young age was an incredible opportunity and experience. I had a huge amount of responsibility, but I thrived on it and couldn't quite believe I was getting paid to put my musical taste to good use. The only downside of working for Geoff was that he had a temper on him. He could get quite short with me at times, and we'd argue.

Around this time, I began to become aware of Tony Hall, who worked in the promotions department. He was extremely dapper and good-looking. He wore mohair suits and was a great jazz aficionado. He was a compère at the Flamingo Club on Wardour Street, a hugely important venue in the development of British jazz and rhythm and blues. At Decca, he was head of Coral Records, which boasted Buddy Holly and the Crickets on its roster, among others.

As part of the promotions department, he worked from an office up in the West End, in Hanover Square. Albert Embankment was nice enough, but Hanover Square was much more happening. I wanted to work there, so when I heard a rumour that Tony was considering offering me a job in promotions, I knew I wanted to take it.

I rang Tony up. 'I hear I'm being considered for the promotions job,' I said.

Tony was a little taken aback at first. 'No,' he replied, before adding, 'but are you interested?'

My emotions roller-coastered from being up to down to up again in a matter of seconds. 'Oh yes,' I said, unable to hide the enthusiasm in my voice.

'Well, you'd better come to my office for an interview then.'

I went over to Hanover Square. Just sitting there, waiting for Tony to appear, I could feel the buzz in the office. Tony ushered me in. I was still only nineteen, but I was confident beyond my years. Our shared passion for music, meanwhile, was clear. I felt the interview was going well, when Tony said, 'If it's OK with you, I'd like to take you over to my apartment. I'd like you to meet my wife.'

My immediate reaction was, *Hello? I've got to please his wife to get the job?* It seemed a strange way to do business, but I was incredibly young and just thought maybe that's the way they do things.

Tony's apartment was spectacular. It was very upmarket and classy – the home of two people who were both cultured and knowledgeable. His wife, Mafalda, was beautiful and voluptuous. When she greeted me and ushered me in, one of the first things I noticed was the Picasso reproduction on the wall.

'Blue Period,' I said, pointing at the print.

'Ah, so you know about art?' Mafalda asked.

'A bit,' I shrugged, but I could tell that she was impressed.

Mafalda took me through to the sitting room, which, like the rest of the apartment, was very classy, the sofa cushions doing that satisfying, expensive, soft *pfft* as I sat down. The conversation we had was different to the one I'd had with Tony. With Mafalda, it was more wide-ranging – a bit about art, a bit about my background. I thought we were getting on quite well and that I was making a good impression, when Mafalda put her tea cup down with a *chink* on its saucer.

'Do you mind if I ask you a personal question?' she asked.

That took me a little by surprise. I wasn't sure where the conversation was going, but in the back of my mind, I had a feeling about what she might ask. I wasn't in a position to say no, not if I wanted the job.

'Of course,' I said, my hands held out wide in a sign of openness. 'Ask me anything you like.'

Mafalda nodded, looked me straight in the eye and asked, 'Tony, are you a homosexual?'

———

Back when I first got the job with Decca, I had needed somewhere to live in London, rather than going back and forth to Eastbourne every day. One of the guys I worked with, George, shared a flat with a friend called Derek in Streatham, south London. It wasn't a big place, and we all had to sleep in the same room. But I had a crush on George, so when he offered to put me up, it felt like a good deal. Unfortunately, once we started living together, that crush disappeared pretty quickly! When George went off on holiday with someone he worked with, I was glad to have a week without him.

When George came back, I asked him how the holiday went. 'It was good,' he said. 'And you'd like Bob, the guy I went with.' George had been invited to a party by a friend of Bob's in the centre of town, somewhere in Bloomsbury, not far from Tottenham Court Road. 'You should come along,' he encouraged me.

When I got to the party, I immediately sensed that it felt different. And then I realised: it was full of gay people. It was a liberating moment. Back in Eastbourne, the only way to meet another gay man was to go cottaging – hanging out around public toilets – which was illegal and potentially dangerous. But here was a party with people and music, where everyone was relaxed and happy to be themselves, without the need to look over their shoulders continually.

Bob was obviously gay, and he was very good-looking. George introduced us, and we immediately hit it off. He told me he lived in Southend, and I started talking about growing up in Eastbourne.

'I didn't realise you lived down there,' Bob said. 'I might be down your way quite soon.'

'OK,' I said, feeling a plan coming together. 'As it happens, I'm going to be back there next week, as I'm taking some time off. So if you're coming that way, come and look me up.'

When Bob came down to the south coast, he did exactly that. The connection I'd felt at the party continued. One thing led to another, and we ended up in bed together. I'd spent so long thinking that I needed to leave Eastbourne to find someone, and here I was, with my first relationship happening in Eastbourne itself.

Bob and I began something of a love affair. He was my first boyfriend, and although we only stayed together a few months, it was one of those early relationships whose influence would ripple through for years to come. I quickly fell in love with him, and in return he was clearly very smitten with me. In the end, work got in the way: I started to get very busy with various projects, and as my career took off, our relationship began to fizzle out. We had the occasional argument – I used to tease him as it made me laugh when he got angry – but we never had a big bust-up or anything like that. We remained friends but stopped seeing each other. It just wasn't meant to last.

In those few months of the affair, though, Bob introduced me properly to gay life in London. I was a bit overawed to begin with. It had never really crossed my mind that there were bars and places where you could go and meet other gay men in more sociable circumstances. I began to understand that there was a whole secret scene out there.

In the East End, there was a number of both gay and gay-and-straight pubs – there was a whole scene of straight guys who wanted to go to bed with gay men, which I never got into. I didn't feel particularly comfortable in gay pubs: I always felt a bit of a stranger in a strange land. But there were other places, too, with a bit more character. There was a club called the Rockingham, which was decked out in tartan wallpaper and pictures of hunting scenes; it was meant to mimic a gentlemen's drinking club. There was another club in Soho called the Ace of Clubs, on Romilly Street. You climbed up a staircase at the side to get in, and once inside you were greeted by a man behind the bar called Harry Heart, a very openly gay guy who'd say, 'Hello, darling.' Harry would always have a huge tumbler of brandy in front of him. You'd buy him another, and he'd top his drink up, saying, 'Thank you, darl, thank you, heart.' He spoke fluent Polari, the gay lingo that Kenneth Williams had made famous on the radio show *Round the Horne* with his Julian and Sandy routine.

After the relationship with Bob ended, I went out with a police-man for a while. I met him in a gay pub in Pimlico. He was ever so handsome, and my jaw dropped when he told me what he did for a living. The newspapers were full of stories about the high-profile prosecutions of gay people like Lord Montagu – such was the notoriety of that case that 'Monty' became slang for 'gay' for a while – and yet here was someone meant to uphold these ridiculous laws but breaking them at the same time.

The policeman took me to the Rockingham, where we both felt a bit more relaxed. He was an extremely nice guy, but a bit boring in bed. The final straw came when we were out on a date in Soho. We were walking down Windmill Street, near Leicester Square, when with an 'Excuse me' he just ran off. I stood there in shock as he ran over to a man who was dealing cards on the street and made to arrest him. I double-blinked as he went into policeman mode, all stiff and serious.

Once the arrest had been made, he came back over.

'Oh my God,' I said. 'What on earth did you do that for?'

'Well, he was gambling on the street,' he said. 'It's not allowed, you know.'

Lots of things aren't allowed, I thought. *Including this relationship.* I realised he wasn't really my cup of tea and broke it off soon after.

As my career in the music business continued, I frequented gay pubs and clubs much less. The music scene had its own circle of venues where I felt much more at home, and as the 1960s began to swing, these became the places to be seen in. I began to find other gay friends in the record industry to hang out with. There was a gang of us who'd go out together, meeting for dinner, and that became my scene instead.

———

In Tony Hall's apartment, Mafalda was waiting for an answer. *So, Tony, are you a homosexual?*

Looking back, it is clear to me that the whole thing was a set-up. I'd already had the interview with Tony, so he knew I could do the job. But he wanted to know about my sexuality and couldn't bring himself to ask me. The jazz club where he compèred, the Flamingo, was quite a hetero environment, and maybe that rubbed off on his thinking – that my being gay might somehow be a hindrance to my doing the job. He didn't have the foresight to see how it might be of benefit, that in fact I could run around and do all kinds of things, that I didn't have any ties and could stay up late with artists.

I glanced around the flat, my eyes settling briefly on the Blue Period Picasso on the wall. I wanted this job. I wanted to be true to myself, too, but it felt like it was fifty–fifty whether I'd be offered the position. I couldn't afford to take the risk.

'No,' I fibbed, turning back to Mafalda, smiling. 'No, I'm not gay.'

Whether Mafalda believed me or not, I'm not sure, but she reported back to Tony. And he gave me the job.

4

The first time I heard 'Love Letters' by Ketty Lester, I knew it was going to be a hit.

Every Monday, we had a listening session. Tony Hall, myself and a couple of the other promotions people would put the kettle on, sit down and listen to all the new music that was coming out on Decca, London American and RCA (though RCA had their own promotions person, Pat Campbell). We'd play all the records that were coming up, the American artists who were going to be released in the UK, and decide which ones we liked and which ones we wanted to work with.

I had just started in the promotions department and was keen to find a song that I could use to make my mark. When the needle dropped down onto the vinyl with its regular hiss and crackle, I wasn't really sure what to expect. What I really wanted was something fast, maybe a bit rock-and-roll, definitely something you could dance to. But 'Love Letters' was completely different.

It started simply, just some piano chords, with a gentle shuffle of drums in the background to accompany them. Even before the singing started, there was a mood, an atmosphere, a feel that drew you in. There was so much space in the record, so much poise in the piano-playing, the gentleness of the rise and fall. And then Ketty Lester began to sing. She had this beautiful soul voice that swept you up as she caressed the words. It was effortless and captivating and charming, all at the same time. Lester wasn't a name yet; she was new and unknown. But there was something about the words and the way she phrased them that drew me in. I knew I had to promote her and could make her a star.

In 1962, plugging was still a relatively new phenomenon. My old headteacher at school was not the only person who thought Elvis was going to be a fad and that the interest in rock and roll would breeze in and then back out again. But that initial burst of attention solidified into something more serious and permanent. People were buying singles and albums, and there was a whole new audience to woo. Getting your artists into the charts was all about getting them on the right radio and television shows. That's where someone like me came in.

The starting point in the early 1960s was to get the record onto the BBC. This was a few years before the birth of Radio 1, and for Ketty Lester, the shows to target were *Housewives' Choice* and *Family Favourites*. Pat Osborne hosted the former; Isobel Barnett and Esther Farmer the latter. They were three old dears, or at least they felt like that to someone barely out of their teens. I would have to take them out to lunch, making an odd foursome of three old biddies and a glamorous young boy. I knew how to charm them, though, having grown up in a home of mainly older women, and we got on like a house on fire. Pat Osborne, in particular, could talk for England. Once she started going on about her husband Bert or her son Nigel, she wouldn't stop. On one occasion we were eating soup, and she sat there, talking away, her spoon hovering underneath her mouth, for the best part of five minutes. In the end, I could take it no more. I reached over, got hold of her arm and gently pushed the soup up to her mouth.

'Pat,' I said, to giggles from the others, 'I think your lunch is going cold.'

I wined and dined the three ladies, talked about how amazing I thought the Ketty Lester record was, and they went back, listened to it and loved it. Theirs weren't the only radio shows to get your records on – *Saturday Club* and *Easy Beat* on a Sunday were also important, depending on the record – but for this particular song, they were the best fit.

Before the arrival of Radio Caroline in 1964, for younger listeners Radio Luxembourg was the main rival to the BBC. At the time, the BBC had a monopoly on radio broadcasting, so any rivals had to find a way to circumvent that. Radio Caroline broadcast from a boat off the East Anglian coast; Radio Luxembourg, meanwhile, had a hugely powerful transmitter that allowed them to broadcast from Europe. They had a studio in London, where some shows were pre-recorded, but most were transmitted from the Grand Duchy. I would be flown out to Luxembourg every so often, where I'd take the DJs out to dinner. Radio Luxembourg was fun but a bit rough and ready at times. I remember being in the studio once when the DJ did the weather forecast. He leaned his head out of the window and said, 'The weather today is good,' and that was the forecast for Europe.

Once you had the record promoted in the right place on the radio, you moved to TV. Sometimes you'd do this in sequence, letting the song catch fire on the radio first. Sometimes you'd try and work on both promotions simultaneously. Jack Good and Philip Jones were the important names here early on. In the late 1950s, Good created the *Six–Five Special*, a Saturday-night pop-music show for the BBC. He then moved to ITV, where he came up with *Oh Boy!*, a more rock-and-roll version of the same idea that went head to head with his original show.

In 1962, *Thank Your Lucky Stars* was the big programme to get your record on. Made by Philip Jones, the show first aired on ITV in 1961 and would run for over two hundred shows, before finishing in 1966. Brian Matthew, Keith Fordyce and Jim

Dale were among the presenters, and the programme featured various artists miming along to their latest singles, as well as a feature called 'Spin-a-Disc', where a panel would review the latest records.

I worked hard for Ketty Lester and arranged for her to appear on *Thank Your Lucky Stars*. I believed in the record, and that must have helped its chances. By the time I'd finished, the song had reached number four in the UK charts, one place higher than it had managed in the US. I was thrilled. A great song was getting the audience it deserved, delivering on the potential that I first heard in that initial Monday-morning meeting.

———

It was while I was doing these radio rounds that I first came across the Beatles, at a BBC show called *Pop Inn*, hosted by Keith Fordyce. As the title suggests, the artists would 'pop in' and chat to Fordyce about their latest record. I'd often be there catching up with other pluggers from the different record labels, swapping stories. On this occasion, I'd gone down with Tony Hall.

At the time of doing the show, the Beatles had already had their first hit with 'Love Me Do' and were there to promote 'Please Please Me'. I was sat in the green room, where the artists would hang out, and the moment they walked in, they lit the place up like thousand-watt light bulbs. John Lennon was the one I was wowed by first. He had this presence and a powerful persona that was difficult to ignore, but also easy to feel a little intimidated by. I started talking to him, and then to George, who was naturally quieter but easier to engage with. I explained what I did and how I was working for London American Records, and then George called Ringo over.

'This guy' – he pointed at me, his voice with that broad Liverpudlian twang – 'he knows all about the records we like, Ringo.' He asked me what I liked at the moment.

'There is a song I love called "If You Gotta Make a Fool of Somebody" by James Ray,' I replied.

George and Ringo's faces lit up. 'We love that song,' George said.

'Well, if you're into that sort of stuff, I'm sure I can get you copies,' I said.

'That would be amazing,' Ringo replied.

I asked them where they lived, and it transpired that the pair of them shared a flat in Green Street that was right by Tony Hall's place. 'That's easy enough,' I said. 'Tell me what you like, and I'll get it to you.'

George and Ringo had a thing for soul and Motown. At the time, Motown went through a label called Oriole Records; a lot of those early songs – 'My Guy' by Mary Wells, 'Do You Love Me' by the Contours, 'Money' by Barrett Strong – came out on that label. The plugger for Oriole was this sweet little man, Ronnie Bell. He was a bit older than the rest of the pluggers, less hip and more middle-aged, but he was so nice that everybody loved him. I had a word with him, and after that I would ply George and Ringo with all the latest American records. They loved that, and I made sure that every time they came back to their flat after another tour or TV show, there'd be a pile of records waiting for them.

Not long after this, I saw the Beatles phenomenon up close and personal. I was looking after Chris Montez, another American singer, who'd had a big hit with a song called 'Let's Dance'. He'd come to the UK to be part of a package tour, which saw a group of artists touring together. Montez and another American singer, Tommy Roe, were the headline acts. The Beatles were further down the bill, on what was their second-ever tour.

That, at least, was how the tour was booked. But by the time the first dates came round, the Beatles were firmly on the rise. The reaction of the crowds to them was markedly different to the reception given to the American stars, and it soon became clear who the headline act should be. So while the tour began with Montez and Roe closing the shows, by the end it was the Beatles who were the final act. Montez, to be fair to him, was OK about it. No artist would like to be in that position, but he didn't get in a mood; it was more a sense of disappointment. I tried to be as understanding as I could, but it was clearly the right call to make.

Especially when you saw the Beatles perform. My God. They were so exciting, just full to the brim with energy and enthusiasm. It was a two-way thing – they fed off the audience, and the audience fed off them. Even through the screams, you could hear that they had great voices and great harmonies. There wasn't much in the way of movement from them: Ringo was stuck behind his drums; John would hold his guitar high; Paul and George were doing their thing. But it only needed the slightest shift from any of them to set the crowd off again.

I loved watching the girls go mental – that sense of abandon, of losing yourself, letting yourself go. A few years earlier, I'd gone to Brighton to see Lonnie Donegan, the man who'd brought skiffle music to the masses. His gigs were full of girls, too, but they used to cheer for him, rather than scream. With the Beatles, there was definitely a sexual element: they all wanted to go to bed with Paul or John or George or Ringo. Even though the girls were young, sex permeated the atmosphere. When it came to the other artists on the bill, like Chris Montez, the interaction with the audience was rather staid by comparison.

———

'I want that car,' Roy Orbison said, looking out of the taxi's window. 'Tony, can you get it for me?'

Apart from plugging records, the other side of the promotions job was looking after the American artists when they came over to the UK, and one of the biggest names I worked with was Roy Orbison. Roy had first shot to fame in 1960, when his song 'Only the Lonely' reached number one. Throughout the early 1960s, the hits kept coming: 'Running Scared', 'Dream Baby', 'In Dreams', 'Falling', 'Blue Bayou', 'It's Over', 'Pretty Woman'. He had one of the most distinctive voices in popular music, so when the opportunity came to take care of him on his British visits, I jumped at the chance.

The first time I looked after Roy he was by himself and doing a series of radio and TV appearances. On other occasions, when he was over here to tour, he came with his wife, Claudette, and one of his young sons, Roy Dewayne. (In a stranger-than-fiction way, Roy Dewayne's younger brother was called Anthony King!) He used to rent an apartment in Dolphin Square, by the river in Pimlico, and over the years I became quite close to the family. Roy himself was just the loveliest of guys: very softly spoken but incredibly sweet-natured. I also got on with and really liked Claudette and Roy Dewayne. One time I asked if I could take Roy Dewayne out for the day, and we had a magical time at the zoo. I remember heading back to Decca's offices, where I had arranged to meet Roy and Claudette, and Roy Dewayne was so tired after all the fresh air and excitement that he'd fallen asleep. I arrived at the record company carrying the sleeping boy, his head resting on my shoulder. Roy and Claudette were touched by that, and it helped us to become friends.

One of the things that Roy liked to do when he was in London was to go out for dinner. It was all on Decca's account, of course, so I made sure he was treated well. On one occasion, he, Claudette and I were driving back from dinner in a taxi to Dolphin Square, when Roy spotted something out of the window on the King's Road. He had a thing about cars, and classic wartime German Mercedes cars in particular: he liked the designs, the running boards and the spotlights. Roy saw one of these Mercedes pull out from a side street and turned to me to say that he wanted to buy it. I leaned forward and rapped on the taxi's partition screen, asking the driver to stop the car.

'Give me a second,' I said, clambering out, thinking, *This is crazy*. I ran down the street, waving my arms, flagging the Mercedes down. I was lucky the driver didn't think I was a mugger or try to run me over. He stopped and wound down the window.

'I'm sorry for bothering you,' I said, leaning down to speak to him, 'but might you be interesting in selling your car?'

The man double-blinked and said, 'Why do you ask?'

'Because' – I pointed back up the road to the taxi, where Roy and Claudette were watching through the back window in amusement – 'because I'm with someone who is desperately keen to buy it.' The driver looked at the taxi and then back at me. 'I'm sure he'd offer you a very good price for it.'

'Hmm,' the driver thought. Then he said, 'Well, I suppose we could talk.'

'Wait there,' I said, and ran back to the taxi. I opened the door. 'Roy, I think he might be interested.'

Roy came out of the cab to join me. The driver double-blinked again when he saw who it was. With his jet-black hair and glasses, Roy was instantly recognisable. 'Are you . . . ?' Roy nodded, and they exchanged numbers.

Later on, I learned from Roy that he had done a deal for the car. The guy sold it to him with a load of spare parts, and Roy had the whole lot shipped back to America.

In 1963, Roy came to the UK to tour with the Beatles – the Beatles' next set of dates after the ones where they'd swapped the headline slot with Chris Montez. In exactly the same way, when the tour was first put together, Roy was the bigger name and the headliner. ('What's a Beatle?' he had famously asked when the idea was put to him.) But by the time the concerts came around, and having seen the reaction to them at the Chris Montez concerts, that needed to change. The tour was rebilled, with Roy and the Beatles co-headlining, the two acts agreeing that the Beatles should close the shows.

Inevitably, there was a bit of rivalry to begin with, but as the shows went on this developed into a huge amount of mutual respect, which would last for decades (indeed, in the 1980s, Roy and George Harrison would work together on the Traveling Wilburys project). And rather than just playing second fiddle, Roy was determined that his show should hit the spot, making him a hard act for the Beatles to follow.

Watching him walk out on stage, that seemed a tall order. The auditoriums across the country were packed with Beatles fans, the excited teenage girls egging each other on into a frenzy, desperate to see their idols. Who was this guy from America with the hair and the glasses? When were the Beatles going to come on? But Roy did something rather magical. Rather than try to out-sing the screams, he instead sang his first number as quietly as he could. The audience stopped screaming and quietened down so that they could hear him. Once they started listening to him, they were enraptured. Roy didn't move much on stage, staying stock still in the centre, but he had a presence and a magnetism, so that all eyes were drawn to him. He had the voice and the songs to keep them hooked. By the time he had finished, with the Beatles getting ready to go on after him, the crowd was on his side. It wasn't an easy thing to do, to match the Beatles at the height of Beatlemania, but somehow Roy managed it.

Such was the fondness and friendship between us that Roy made me an offer. How would I like to come and work for him in America? It seemed a crazy, preposterous idea. I loved all things American, and the chance to work for him and live over there seemed like a fantastic opportunity. But at the same time, Roy lived in Nashville rather than New York or Los Angeles. Would I really fit in there? Being gay on the East or West Coast was one thing, but in the home of country music? I was keen, but looking back perhaps it was for the best that I didn't really understand how to get a work permit for the US. I failed to sort out my visa, and the opportunity came and went.

Over the next few years, this great singer of tragic songs was hit by tragedy himself. His marriage to Claudette ran into difficulties and they separated, before later getting back together again. Worse, however, was to come. First, Claudette was killed in a motorbike accident, and then sweet little Roy Dewayne and his brother died in a house fire. I was devastated when I heard the news. Roy was the loveliest gentleman and didn't deserve any of this.

In 1989, when the Rolling Stones were inducted into the Rock and Roll Hall of Fame, I met Barbara Orbison, Roy's second wife. Roy had recently passed away, and I wanted to offer my condolences.

'You don't know me,' I said, as I went up, 'but my name is Tony King and I . . .'

'Tony King!' Barbara's face lit up. 'Your name is a legend in our house. You're the man who helped Roy to buy his Mercedes. That was one of his favourite stories,' she told me. 'It was one of his favourite things to tell people.'

A few years later, the BBC were making a documentary about Roy and Barbara, and they asked if I would be in it. I was honoured, and Johnny Cash and I spoke about Claudette and the boys. Illustrious company. When they asked me about the fire, I closed my eyes, because I could remember hearing about it so distinctly.

It was a fitting film for a great man. When it was broadcast, I watched it with another great man, Charlie Watts, in his kitchen. After it had finished, we sat there for a moment in silence. Then Charlie turned to me and, in his deadpan way, said, 'Well, you were a lot more interesting than Bono.'

——

Another artist I chaperoned in this period was the mighty Brenda Lee. I loved working with Brenda. She was great fun to be with and just brilliant on stage – her dedication and professionalism were like nothing I'd ever seen before. She might have been relatively young at this point, but she knew exactly what she wanted.

When she came over to the UK, she had a band, Sounds Incorporated, which she had auditioned and recruited specifically to play with her over here. I remember watching her put the group through their paces: if these musicians thought this was just a jobbing gig for some American star passing through, they were seriously mistaken. She made them *work*. Brenda wanted everything just so, but not in a diva way. She was more than willing to put the hard yards in, and expected everyone else to do the same.

'Where did you learn to do all that?' I asked her, after one set of rehearsals.

'Paris,' she replied. Brenda explained that she had spent some time there with the French singer Gilbert Bécaud. She had observed him closely, learning from his professionalism and incorporating it into her own career. I remember that when we did the TV show *Thank Your Lucky Stars*, she knew where all the camera marks were. The director, Philip Jones, told her where he wanted her to look and perform from, and she did it instinctively.

Not every singer was quite as professional as Brenda. She was booked to appear on one show alongside Gene Vincent, the rocker. Vincent was a bit wild: it was no secret that he liked to drink, sometimes to excess. This show was one of those occasions. He was so out of it that he pissed all over the floor in the corridor outside the dressing rooms. Brenda was due on stage, so she opened her door, looking stunning in a voluminous dress and matching high-heeled satin shoes.

'Oh my God,' she said, looking at me. 'What's with all this water on the floor?'

I thought quickly. 'It's one of the fire extinguishers,' I explained. 'I think it must have leaked.'

Brenda harrumphed and hitched her skirt up. 'Well, somebody better get it cleaned up.' She tiptoed through and went off to perform, unaware of what her beautiful shoes had just waded through.

Brenda was as fun off stage as she was professional on it. She had a boyfriend, Ronnie, back home, but wanted someone to go out with while she was over in London. That someone was me. One time, I was working in the office, when she rang up and asked, 'Will you go to a movie with me?' I looked over at Tony Hall, who asked where I was going, and I explained. He was fine with it – that was the job – so I took Brenda to a lunchtime showing of the Chubby Checker film *Let's Twist Again* in Piccadilly. Brenda, it turned out, was the most fun person to go to the cinema with. She sang along to all of the songs at the top of her voice, her very recognisable Brenda Lee tones echoing around the auditorium. She was a great dancer, too, and I got her to teach me all of the latest moves: the Mashed Potato, the Watusi, the Pony. If you're going to learn, you might as well learn from the best!

Every artist had different things they liked to do. Johnny Tillotson, who had a huge hit with 'Poetry in Motion', just wanted to eat fish and chips. There was a posh fish-and-chip shop in South Kensington that he fell in love with, and we ate there time and again. Della Reese, famous for huge American hits such as 'Don't You Know?', loved to go shopping. I loved Della – a heavenly, voluptuous, African American woman who was an absolute force of nature. When she told me she wanted to go shopping, I asked where she wanted to go.

'Harrods,' she replied.

Harrods in the early 1960s was not exactly cut out for someone like Della. It was a bit like that scene in *Pretty Woman* with Julia Roberts in the clothes store, except with an additional layer of racism slipped in. As soon as we walked through the doors, I could feel the staff looking at us. The *vendeuse* appeared, as if out of nowhere, with one of those cut-glass offers of 'Can I help you?' that suggested anything but. Della either didn't notice or couldn't care less.

'We're just looking,' she said, as she glided past and started flicking through the rails for something to try on. She pulled out a mustard-coloured trouser suit and asked, 'Can I try this on?'

'Of course, Madam,' the *vendeuse* said, all stiffness.

The *vendeuse* and I waited for Della to change. When she appeared again, the trouser suit was fit to bursting. Her bottom and breasts were giving new meaning to the word 'stretched' as they squeezed into the outfit. Della stood there, posing and looking at herself in the mirror.

'I think it looks very good on Madam,' the *vendeuse* said.

'Really?' Della gave her a look. 'Because I think it looks like shit.' And with that she sashayed back into the changing room, hand on hip.

———

It was a crisp, chilly weekday morning, as my taxi made its way to Heathrow. I glanced at my watch again: I was late. Around us, the traffic bumped and ground its way forward. Above us, I could see the planes descending to land. It was my worst nightmare. I was meant to meet my latest charges in arrivals, but if I wasn't there, where would they go? How would I find them? How would they find me?

I opened the car door even before the taxi had pulled to a stop and was out, running and dodging between the passengers wheeling their suitcases on trolleys. I was heading for the exit door, through which everyone was coming out, when I double-blinked. Sat on a bench was a trio of young Black women, all beautifully posed. They had their luggage arranged around them, legs all neatly aligned, hair piled up high to the heavens. They looked a million dollars. They were Ronnie, Estelle and Nedra – better known as the Ronettes.

Out of all the American artists I looked after in the early 1960s, the Ronettes were probably the group I enjoyed looking after the most. As Ronnie said in her memoir, they liked to have fun, and I took my job very seriously. There was a period when Estelle was dating George Harrison, and a whole group of us would go dancing every night, continuing until the sun came up in the morning. We'd go to discos and places like Dolly's on Jermyn Street, which was this wonderful basement bar that would stay open all hours. I'd got all my moves, which I'd been taught by Brenda Lee, and would be up there with the girls having a whale of a time. The music they played was great, too. I remember hearing this one song I loved and asking George what it was. He went over to ask the DJ, and returned with the record.

'It's "Mockingbird" by Charlie and Inez Foxx,' he said, handing it over. 'The DJ said I could have it.'

I asked George to sign it for me, and I still have it in my collection somewhere. The fact that I managed to keep hold of it that night was something of a minor miracle. We got back to Green Street, where George and Ringo lived in the flat near to Tony Hall, at six or seven in the morning. Around us, people were leaving their houses and going to work, while we were all smashed and giggling, still full of the night before. Once in the apartment, the giggling and shrieking continued. We pulled everything we could find out of the cupboards and cooked. I'd call it breakfast, but it was more of a drunken feast. There were eggs, there were processed peas, there was everything. But we were so hungry that nobody minded, and we ate the lot. By the time we'd finished, the kitchen looked as though a tornado had ripped through it.

At that point, everyone who was a musician got to crash and go to bed. I, however, had to go to work. My head spinning and my stomach weighed down with food, I made my way over to the office. I was slumped behind my desk, staring into space, when Tony Hall appeared.

'Tony,' he said, snapping me awake. 'Work.'

'The thing is,' I said, 'I haven't been to bed yet.' I explained what had happened, and by the time I'd finished, he had a huge grin on his face. He was relieved, I think, that I'd had to go through all that rather than him. He let me off.

Perhaps the most memorable night with the Ronettes came in early 1964, when Tony hosted a party for the Beatles. It was the night before the band were due to fly to America for the first time, to make their historic appearance on *The Ed Sullivan Show* that heralded Beatlemania properly making its way across the Atlantic. The Beatles had released a few records in the US that hadn't done much, but after 'I Want to Hold Your Hand' went to number one, all those other songs reappeared and climbed back up the charts.

The Beatles themselves were hugely excited about the trip. They were a bit like schoolboys about to go on a school outing. They didn't know – no one really did – what would await them when they landed. The Ronettes were all at the party, along with producer and songwriter Phil Spector; Estelle and Nedra, I think, went back to the US on the same flight as the Beatles. I can't remember whether Jane Asher was there with Paul, but John came with Cynthia, his then wife. She was touchingly sweet and incredibly kind, and was constantly taking care of John: 'Can I get you a glass of water?' – that kind of thing.

It was such a warm atmosphere. There was a sense of excitement, the feeling of being on the cusp of something. And the Ronettes, as always, brought the fun. The moment I remember most clearly came when someone put on 'Heatwave' by Martha Reeves and the Vandellas, and Ronnie started singing along to it. George and John, I recall, just sat there, mouths agape at this beautiful, clear, American soul voice. Note perfect, word perfect – wonderful. It was a moment within a moment, and I stood there, drink in hand, listening and watching on, knowing what a privilege it was to be there.

5

'This is going to be their next single. I'd love to know what you think of it . . .'

It was 1965, and I was sat in the office of a young, good-looking, sharply dressed music supremo. I'd always thought I had youth on my side, but this was someone even younger, yet he was already about as successful as it was possible to get. So when he called me up and asked if I'd be interesting in working for him, I agreed to go and see him.

By now, I'd been working in the music business for seven years, and with Tony Hall for several of those. It was a good gig – a great one, in fact. I had a decent boss, worked with some amazing artists and was living it up. Why on earth would I want to change any of that?

But then the needle came down on the acetate. There was the briefest bit of crackle and then, *whoomph*, one of the most iconic riffs in the whole of rock and roll ripped through the speakers.

Da da da-da-dah . . .

The song finished. Andrew Loog Oldham lifted the needle off the record and turned to look at me.

'Well?' he asked. 'Would you like to come and work here?'

If someone had played you an advance copy of 'Satisfaction' by the Rolling Stones at your job interview, what would you have said?

The first time I saw the Rolling Stones, I have to confess that I wasn't that knocked out. I had been invited by Chrissie Shrimpton, who was the assistant to Geoff Milne, the London American Records label manager whom I'd worked for before Tony Hall poached me for promotions. Chrissie was the sister of Jean Shrimpton, the model who would become one of the faces of the decade. At the time, she had a partner who would go on to become similarly iconic: Mick Jagger. When she invited me along to see her boy-friend's band, I did so more out of duty than anything else.

The Stones were playing at the Scene Club in Ham Yard, Soho. Even though it was a tiny club, it was still only half full. Compared to some of the gigs I'd seen with the Beatles, with packed auditoriums going crazy, it all felt a bit flat by comparison. The Stones themselves were a bit rough around the edges. When their first single, 'Come On', had come out, they'd had an audition to play at the BBC, which they'd failed, with Mick Jagger's singing singled out for criticism.

I was a big Beatles fan at this point. I loved them partly because they were inspired by early pop records, by Motown and things like that. They were a pop band. The Stones, by contrast, were a blues band, coming from a different tradition altogether. It took me a while to get into that, but then I became a convert, and then a fan, and then a devotee. From that point on, I loved their music, who they were, what they stood for. Even before 'Satisfaction', 'The Last Time' was a great record. So was 'Little Red Rooster'. I began to understand that I was appraising Mick all wrong.

Back at Ham Yard, I was yet to get this, yet to be convinced. The Stones had something, but I still didn't understand what it was. After the show, Chrissie introduced me to Mick. I don't know if he was just acting cool, but he didn't seem particularly thrilled to meet me. In fact, he came across as though he couldn't care less.

He was very offhand, and I don't suppose that helped in forming my early view of the band.

But as the Stones grew in stature, I got to know their dynamic young manager, Andrew Loog Oldham. When I first met him, he was doing freelance publicity for a singer called Mark Wynter. Wynter was on Pye Records and was managed by a guy called Ray Mackender. Mackender was gay and had a lovely boyfriend called Jerry. I used to go round to their flat in Great Cumberland Street, and that was where I first met Andrew. He was sat in the corner, making notes about Wynter. Right from the start, I could see he was committed, and I had a sense that he might go far.

From there, he was picked up by Brian Epstein to do some publicity work for the Beatles. He used to come into the office to see Tony Hall and recognised me from that initial meeting. We became friends and would go out for coffee at the Café de la Paix, in Hanover Square, off Regent Street. He introduced me to Sheila, his girlfriend, who went on to become his wife. Andrew and I were similar people, with a similar passion for music, and we were both younger than most of our contemporaries in the business.

Andrew moved on from promotion to management and took the Stones under his wing. His eye for publicity helped to shape the group's image, and his ear for music helped to build the band's sound, guided by his production. As the Stones began to grow, both in popularity and notoriety, he asked me if I'd come and work for him. The first time he asked, I said no. I was happy working for Tony Hall, and Andrew was so young it felt too much of a risk to jump ship. But then he played me that acetate of 'Satisfaction', and the offer was impossible to turn down.

———

Andrew's office was in Ivor Court, just off Baker Street. Technically, it wasn't meant to be an office and was actually registered as an apartment. In order to continue the conceit, he put a single bed in my office, just in case anyone ever asked. It was meant to be there for show, but the Stones began to make use of it. Early on when I was working there, I got into the office one morning and put the lights on, only to discover a blinking and bleary Keith Richards staring out at me from under the covers.

'Oh, hello,' I said, not quite sure what to say. 'How are you?'

Classic Keith, he groaned and said, 'Ooh, OK.'

'Do you want me to wake you up later with a cup of tea?' I asked.

'Yeah, all right,' Keith said, turning back over.

I switched the lights off and shut the door behind me, not quite sure what I was to do for the rest of the morning. This sort of thing didn't happen back at Decca. I left him until about one o'clock, at which point I knocked gently and brought him a cup of tea. Having woken him up and then let him sleep, he was now less growly and much more friendly. Incredibly sweet, in fact. We talked, and I still remember it as being one of the nicest conversations, just the two us together. I asked him about the Stones' trip to America and watched as his eyes lit up.

'Oh, it was wonderful,' he grinned.

I settled into my chair. 'I'm dying to know.'

I soaked it all up, having had a long-standing love of all things American. He really came alive talking about their trip to Chess Studios in Chicago. From the way he became animated, you could see and sense his love for the blues, and how important it was for him to have been where all those records he loved had been recorded.

The first time I met Mick in the office was equally memorable. I was working away at my desk when I heard the front door go.

Even before I saw him, I heard his unmistakeable voice floating down the hallway.

'Chrissie has gone and locked me out of the flat.'

That sounds like Mick Jagger, I thought. Sure enough, his head appeared around the door.

'Chrissie's gone and locked me out of the flat,' he repeated. 'Who are you, by the way?'

I put the kettle on and we got talking, the offhand nature of our previous meeting long forgotten.

When I started working for the Stones, it was very much about the three of them: Mick, Keith and Andrew. Brian Jones was a bit of a fallen angel. He was the original leader of the band and had come up with the group's name, but Andrew had the instinct to see that Mick was the person to shape the band around. As my mum used to say, he has got so much life in him. And so, by the time I came along, the balance of power had already shifted. Andrew, Mick and Keith used to gang up on Brian a little. There was the time they all went off to Morocco, and Brian got sick and Keith made off with his girlfriend, the model Anita Pallenberg, which was all a bit awkward.

He was a strange mix, Brian. He had these angelic looks, this beautiful hair, a lovely smile. But there was a devilish streak to him as well, particularly with regard to how he treated his girlfriends. Just before he died, when he was up in court for possession of cannabis and looked set to go to prison, I remember thinking that he didn't look so good any more. He seemed a bit sad, a little run down. When he used to come into the office and have a cup of tea with me, he was always incredibly softly spoken, fey and whispery, at complete odds with Mick, Keith and Andrew.

Charlie Watts, meanwhile, became one of my dearest friends. His wife, Shirley, was a sculptress and had just come out of the

Royal Academy. She was into horses, dogs and other things, so their lives didn't revolve around music and London so much. It wasn't long before they left the capital to live in Lewes, in Sussex.

To begin with, though, they lived in a flat down the corridor from the office. When I first started working for Andrew, they were away. I remember seeing this cat in the corridor. It was limping around and clearly wasn't well. I asked Andrew about it, and he said, 'Oh, that is Louise, Charlie and Shirley's cat. Can you take it to the vet for me?'

I bundled the cat up and took it down to the vet, who took one look at Louise, shook his head and said he'd have to put her down. I looked down at this poor, sweet creature looking back up at me with a pair of sad, sorrowful eyes. I couldn't agree to that. It didn't seem like a good harbinger for the start of my Rolling Stones career to be the person who facilitated having Charlie's cat put down.

'Is there nothing I can do?' I asked.

The vet paused. 'Well, there is someone called Mr Butt in Gloucester Place. He can sometimes save creatures, if he's still going.'

I scooped Louise up, caught another cab and headed straight over. Mr Butt, the miracle vet, was still working and, having looked at Louise, said he could help.

'She's got a shattered back leg,' he said, after inspecting her. Somehow he put the limb back together, like a jigsaw puzzle, with wire and plaster. He didn't come cheap: I remember the operation cost me twenty-five pounds, which was a huge amount of money at the time.

When Charlie and Shirley returned, they were delighted with what I'd done. Charlie took one look at me and said to Shirley, 'I think he is the gayest person I have ever met in my entire life.'

But they took to me after that first act of kindness. I'd grown quite fond of Louise by this point and asked if I could visit her. 'Anytime you like,' they said.

When they moved down to Lewes, they invited me to come down and stay over. And when I got there, guess who appeared and sat on my bed? Later, they bought a lovely farm in the Languedoc, in France. I went to stay with them there, too, and again a familiar creature would come and sleep on my bed. 'She always knows when you're in the house,' Shirley said. It was one of the nicest things, waking up in the morning and seeing Louise's tilted face, ready to greet me.

———

Working for Andrew and the Stones in the mid-1960s was a heady cocktail of music, drugs, alcohol and excess. The days seemed to lurch from drinking and getting stoned to recovering from drinking and getting stoned, and then drinking and getting stoned again.

Andrew knew how to live well and make the most of the moment. He was a leading light, a trailblazer. He had great fashion sense and was always drop-dead chic in the best clothes, the best suits. Looking back, I think I was a bit in awe of him. I had a bit of a crush: it was incredibly easy to fall for him because of his success, his influence. He seemed impressive in every way: as well as the latest fashion trends, he knew the best restaurants to eat at and had a chauffeur to drive him around. He had the sort of larger-than-life personality that made him someone you just wanted to hang around with.

Drugs played a part in that. In those days, it was about dope and hash. Later on, it became more about acid, and after that it was coke, but in the mid-1960s, dope was more where it was at. West Indian and Moroccan hash were popular. The latter was quite the favourite. You'd light it, burn it, then crumble it into a joint. I used to get it from a couple of girls near my office. They were call girls, as it happened, and incredibly nice and helpful. I used to score off them, picking up a lump of hash and keeping it in my office drawer, along with the skins. I became quite the joint-roller. Some of my friends were ridiculously talented in that department: they would roll what I called a 'trident', which had three joints in the main stem. I sometimes made huge joints – six skins – but mostly I just made regular ones. I always made sure that the hash I got was good, so people could get properly stoned. Andrew had this euphemism he liked to use – 'I think we need to talk to the promotions department about that' – which was my cue to start rolling.

It seems strange to say it now, but Keith wasn't such a big fan of smoking at first. He had a girlfriend called Linda Keith, who was a very attractive north London Jewish girl. One night, I was over at Andrew's flat in Montpellier Square. Linda was there, too, and we all smoked a joint together. When Keith arrived later on, he immediately smelled the dope.

'You haven't been turning my girlfriend on, have you?' he asked me.

He wasn't best pleased, but he soon got over it. And the next thing you knew, he was smoking up a storm like everybody else.

———

Andrew had a Rolls-Royce that I helped to get for him. What with that and the Roy Orbison story, it sounds like I was some sort of car dealer, but the two events weren't connected. The Rolls came through a man called Terry Doran, who used to be in partnership with Brian Epstein, the Beatles' manager. They had a company called Bridor Cars (a combination of their names). Terry sold Rolls-Royces, but the waiting list was a mile long, so I said to Andrew that I would see what I could do. I went to see Terry and pulled every favour I could think of, and suddenly Andrew was moved up the list and a car was available. It was a beautiful thing – a Rolls-Royce Phantom Five, to which Andrew added dark windows so people couldn't see in. Inside, it was decked out with pink lighting. Andrew also had a record player fitted so he could listen to music as his chauffeur drove him round.

Of course, having helped Andrew acquire the Rolls, I got to accompany him. One of his favourite things to do was to get stoned and listen to music in the back of the car. Once, we were all at a recording session, when Andrew turned to me and said, 'Do you fancy going to Brighton?' We piled in, put the records on and got completely stoned for the journey. At about four in the morning, we got to Brighton. We crawled out of the car, crunched down the pebbles to look at the sea, then got back in and drove home.

On another occasion, Andrew and I went to London Airport to pick up an associate of Allen Klein's who was coming over from the States (by this point Klein had been brought in to help on the business side). Andrew told me to make a few joints to greet the guy with, to give him a warm welcome. 'Make sure they're strong,' he told me.

We met this associate off the plane, piled back into the Rolls, and the three of us smoked this joint. It was strong stuff, and we all got obliterated. After a while, I realised this guy hadn't said anything at all. I turned to him and asked, 'So, how are you feeling?'

He just stared back at me. 'I am out of my fucking *mind*,' he replied.

Music and dope went hand in hand. One time, I was staying at Tony Hall's flat for a few nights, when the phone went at midnight. It was Andrew, asking me to come into the office. I took a taxi over to Ivor Court, where he was sat with all the curtains drawn. He had just been sent a copy of *Pet Sounds*, the new album by the Beach Boys, and wanted me to listen to it with him. The album is brilliant anyway, but hearing it for the first time, completely stoned, was an amazing experience. The same thing happened when he got hold of the first Mamas and the Papas album. Andrew had been to LA and had come back evangelical about the album: 'Listen to *this*.' There's a moment in the middle of 'California Dreamin'', the instrumental section, where it shifts up a gear. Even now, when I hear it, it still has echoes of that first, stoned *woah* moment.

———

By the mid-1960s, *Ready Steady Go!* was *the* British TV show for a group to appear on, the perfect vehicle for the Stones to strut their stuff. The camera loved Mick, and Mick loved the camera. The programme's directors were Vicki Wickham and Michael Lindsay-Hogg, and they were a great double act. Vicki was the ideas person who made things happen, while Michael was all about the visuals. He was a charismatic, creative cinematographer who would go on to have a long relationship with the Stones. Years later, when I was working for John Lennon in the States, I remember watching the Stones on one of the American Saturday-night shows. The band were surrounded by soap suds and bubbles, and Mick was in the thick of it, dancing away in his gold lamé suit. It was hilarious and ridiculous and brilliant and iconic all at the same time – another Michael Lindsay-Hogg masterclass.

Ready Steady Go! had a freedom and an edge to it. It was broadcast live on a Friday night and was a great place to hang out. Even when we didn't have a band on, Andrew, I and others would go along. It didn't feel like work; you went there to have fun. The team behind the programme were all quite young and relatively inexperienced, which meant that things were a bit chaotic: there'd be people dancing everywhere, cameras getting in the way of the shots, but that was part of its charm. It worked because it came across on screen as though all these people were having a really great time, and that's because we were.

I remember the New Year shows as being particularly raucous, and the programme wasn't afraid to try different things. On one occasion, they did an amazing Motown special, hosted by Dusty Springfield (Vicki was the driving force behind making that happen, if I remember rightly). Beyond the music, there'd be pieces about fashion and interviews with comedians like Peter Cook and Dudley Moore. Mick and Michael worked well together. I remember a Rolling Stones special in which the band came on to perform 'Paint It Black', and Michael made the lighting darker and darker, bringing out this sinister undertone.

———

'Here, Tony. Do you know who that is over there?'

It was another night in the Ad Lib, a small but happening nightclub above the Prince Charles cinema, just off Leicester Square. It was a club with strong links to the Beatles, somewhere they would often come and hang out. George and John went there after they took LSD for the first time, having had it slipped into their tea by a dentist at a dinner party. As one did back then.

This particular evening I was with Cilla Black. Cilla I'd known ever since she first became famous. As a fellow Liverpudlian who'd just made it, she was often around when the Beatles were about. She was great fun, had this gorgeous dirty laugh and a wicked sense of humour, and she loved to dance, which all worked for me. We quickly became firm friends.

On this occasion, Cilla was pointing at someone sat at a table opposite. Although it was dark in the club, there was something striking about the sharpness of this person's features that gave her away almost immediately. I gasped. It was Christine Keeler, one of the most iconic figures of the early 1960s. Now I adored Christine. I couldn't get enough of her after the story broke about her relationship with the politician John Profumo. It dominated the headlines, culminating in her court appearances alongside Mandy Rice-Davies, and I would buy every edition of every paper to get the latest picture of her.

To me, Christine oozed style and class. Insouciance. Elan. There was something about the way she would turn up to court in a limo with her friend, Paula Hamilton-Marshall, and stroll in looking like a million dollars. She had this mane of immaculately coiffured hair, wore the right skirts and suits that were nipped in at the waist, and always had a cigarette on the go. Despite everything she was going through, she carried herself with grace and glamour. She was like Rita Hayworth to me. I worshipped her.

I had already been around all kinds of people in my life, had worked with so many of the most famous musicians on the planet. I didn't usually get starstruck, but somehow with Christine Keeler it was different. Here was an idol, in the flesh. I couldn't just go over and introduce myself. Instead, Cilla and I hatched a plan.

We'd get up and dance, surreptitiously shuffling our way round the dance floor until we were close to where Christine was sitting and could sneak a proper look at her.

I don't know if Christine knew what we were doing. I suspect it was one of those plans where you think you're being smart and subtle, but in fact it's obvious to everyone what you're up to. But if Christine knew, she never let on. She stayed there, impassive, as dramatically and elegantly beautiful in the flesh as she'd been in the newspaper photographs. To be that close to her, even fleetingly, was enough.

Everyone has a different memory of when the swinging sixties began, but for me the Profumo affair was a stepping stone between the politics of the past and the glamour and style that the decade would usher in and become famous for. Conservative prime minister Harold Macmillan used to have a slogan: 'You've never had it so good.' Early in the 1960s, I remember taking a jazz boat down the Thames. Acts like Acker Bilk and Ken Colyer would play, and the boat would take you down to Dreamland, an amusement park in Margate. You got out, had fun, then headed back to London. By the time you arrived, everyone was pissed. On this particular trip, someone had a placard featuring an edited-down version of Macmillan's slogan. The 'so good' had disappeared, so it now just read, 'You've never had it.' In a way, that summed up where my generation was. We'd grown up in the aftermath of the war, with rationing and patched-up clothes. Money was tight. Holidays were about going to Margate, sitting in the first-floor restaurant of the Home and Colonial store and looking out to sea.

When I was coming of age, everything about Elvis – the music, his moves – was new. But now so was the fashion, the photography, the art – Mary Quant, John Stevens, Terence Donovan, Ossie

71

Clark, David Bailey, Vidal Sassoon. No one was copying or following what had gone before. The culture that was being created was fresh and distinctive, and everything fed off everything else. The rock stars mixed with the hairdressers, who mixed with the dressmakers, who mixed with the photographers. If you went out to dinner, you'd bump into all sorts. That cross-fertilisation was central to what made 1960s culture what it was. All of a sudden, it was as though London had burst from black and white into Technicolor.

Ossie Clark's fashion shows were a good example of that. The whole of the 1960s crowd would congregate there. Bianca Jagger and Pattie Boyd would be modelling; the Beatles, the Stones, David Hockney and his impossibly beautiful boyfriend, Peter Schlesinger, would be sat in the audience. It was all very relaxed, convivial and buzzing.

I became good friends with Ossie. He and Celia lived in Powis Square, Notting Hill – the setting, I think, of that famous Hockney painting of them and the cat. The clothes he designed were out of this world. Celia was a fabulous fabric designer; a lot of her fabrics were inspired by Léon Bakst, who designed for the Ballets Russes. Ossie was clever: he used to cut 'on the bias', which is quite difficult to do. He made these wonderful snakeskin jackets that were very close-fitting. He used to give his models a joint and a glass of champagne before they went on, so they were always, if not quite out of it, just tipsy enough to be fun, unpredictable and memorable.

Fashion had always been a big deal for me. Right from Elvis's early days, I'd try to dress like him. By the time I went on that jazz boat, the trend was for long, oversized sweaters. I remember taking a jumper of mine, putting it on the washing line and then nailing it to the garden shed to make it stretch. I followed the designers, was there when Carnaby Street was taking off, then moved on to the King's Road when that was the happening place to be. It was there, in a boutique called Granny Takes a Trip, that I bumped into Brian and Keith one Saturday afternoon. They had been shopping for clothes, and Brian, in his fey, slightly faded voice, asked me if I liked his new shirt.

'Where is it?' I asked. Brian was wearing layer after layer, and eventually he reached down and showed me a scrap of garment at least three layers down.

'It's great,' I said.

The following night, the Stones were appearing on *Sunday Night at the Palladium*. The band hadn't wanted to appear, but Andrew was insistent. That Sunday was a strange day – probably because it was the day I had my first acid trip, which I took with Denny Cordell, who managed and produced the Moody Blues. I was there with him and his children, his babies rolling around on the bed while we were tripping.

In the evening, I watched the Stones on TV. Keith's and Brian's outfits looked familiar. Then I realised: they were still in the same clothes I'd seen them wearing in Chelsea the previous afternoon. Their dishevelled appearance and performance made sense: they'd obviously been out all night. Whether they'd actually managed to go to bed or not, who knows?

Looking back over this period, I have so many amazing memories of nights out in the Ad Lib, the Cromwellian and the Scotch of St James. Among these, one particular evening stands out: an impromptu party back at Andrew's that included myself, Mick, Keith and Paul McCartney, among others. Someone put on a Supremes record. I loved them, and before I knew it, I was doing my best Diana Ross impression, lip-syncing to cheers from the rest of the crowd. Before they realised what was happening, I'd dragged Mick and Keith over to join me, the Flo and Mary to my Diana, while Paul McCartney watched on, mouth agape.

In the 1970s, when I was working with John Lennon, I remember him asking me one day about Elton John. At the time, Elton wasn't in the best of places. John remarked that Elton was probably going through his 'Help' period.

'What do you mean by that?' I asked.

'Well, we had it when we were famous and it was getting on top of us, and that is why I wrote "Help".' John sang me the words, his lyrics about keeping your feet on the ground, the 'please' needed when asking for help. 'It was a blast,' he remembered, 'but because you were mixing that blast with alcohol and drugs, it became a bit of a delicate cocktail.'

I think the mid-1960s were somewhat like that for Andrew. He was very good at keeping his cards close to his chest, but from his reaction to albums like *Pet Sounds*, you knew he was a sensitive soul. As the Rolling Stones got bigger and bigger – 'Satisfaction' hitting number one in the States, for example – a lot of pressure bore down on his young shoulders. In his memoir, Andrew described his struggles with depression and difficulties with sleeping. I remember he'd disappear for days, going off to Switzerland to try different sleep cures, to allow himself to rest.

As the Stones' success continued to spiral upwards, Andrew had the business sense to bring Allen Klein on board; ultimately, he would go on to replace Andrew as manager. The band, too, would eventually move on from Andrew's production. His style in the studio was very much to fly by the seat of his pants, but he made some great records: 'Have You Seen Your Mother, Baby, Standing in the Shadow', 'Get Off of My Cloud', for example. He had an amazing ear for music, yet he wasn't a traditional producer in the way that, say, Jimmy Miller was, who would go on to produce the Stones. Whether it was business or in the studio, Andrew's style was freewheeling. It made him fun and exciting to be around, and for that moment in time, it was exactly what the Stones needed.

But how and why things changed, and why Andrew and the Stones parted company, I can't say exactly. Because by that point, I had moved on myself, having accepted a job working for George Martin – a decision that would shape the best part of the next decade of my life.

6

In June 1967, I made my way to the EMI studio to be in the audience at a very special TV performance. The show was *Our World*, the first-ever international satellite production. Pulling together broadcasts from around the world, the programme was seen by a global audience of somewhere between 400 and 700 million people.

At the studio, the audience was much smaller and more select. Mick Jagger was there. So was Keith Richards. So were Marianne Faithful, Keith Moon, Eric Clapton and Graham Nash. I'd gone along with Pattie Boyd. I'd known Pattie for years, right from when she first met George Harrison. Although I'd known George back when he was dating Estelle from the Ronettes, it was through Pattie that I became proper friends with him. I would go down and stay with them at their house in Esher at the weekend. It was always very chilled and relaxed. They used to make these delicious shepherd's pies, I seem to remember.

This June day at the studio we'd all done our bit to look the part. Mick had this incredible shirt on, with a painting of someone smoking a cigarette on its back. I really wanted that shirt. It was a bit like when I went to see Cream at the Saville Theatre, and Eric was wearing this most fabulous cream suit, which I coveted as well. That was also the night when Pattie and Eric met. I was in a box with her and George, and we all went backstage to see Eric. I asked Eric where he got his suit, and he told me it was from Allsopp, Brindle and Boyle on the King's Road. The next day, I went straight there and asked Mr Brindle, the tailor, to make me another cream double-breasted suit. Eric and I had similar tastes in clothes. On another occasion he saw a pair of Red Wing boots I was wearing and asked where I'd got them. A few weeks later, I went into the shop, and the owner said Eric Clapton had just been in. *Of course he has*, I thought.

For once, Eric, Mick, Keith and the others weren't the ones up on stage. Instead, it was the Beatles, who were performing their new song, 'All You Need Is Love'. The studio was decked out with flowers and balloons. John, Paul and George were all sat on stools, with Ringo behind on the drums. Off to one side was a brass section. Unfortunately, because of the technology of the time, the performance was shown in black and white, but in the studio, the full colour was something else. The song's message was simple, straightforward and chimed with the idealism of the times. What I didn't know then was that in a few short years, I'd be finding out for myself whether love was, in fact, all you needed.

———

I think it was Peter Sullivan who originally contacted me about working for George Martin and AIR Music. He was one of the company's four partners, and he asked me if I'd be interested in coming over for an interview. AIR was an independent production company, one of the first, I think, to set up in the UK. Those involved had decided that they could make better money if they owned their own business. If such a company was unusual at the time, so was having their own promotions person.

The four partners in AIR Music all brought with them their own roster of talent. Peter looked after Tom Jones and Engelbert Humperdinck. John Burgess made Manfred Mann. And then there were the people I'd be working for – George Martin and Ron Richards. Ron made the Hollies' records. George produced various acts; among them were Roger Cook and Roger Greenaway, who went out under the name of David and Jonathan, and Cilla Black, but obviously his most important client was the Beatles.

George was simply the most delightful man to work with and for. I found him kind, thoughtful, creative, focused. He had a beautifully modulated voice, and I always remember my surprise on meeting his father. Like my dad, he was a carpenter and had a much more ordinary, blokey voice.

'How on earth did you get to speak like that?' I asked George afterwards.

'When I was in the RAF,' George explained, 'I schooled myself to speak correctly.'

The Beatles and Cilla used to tease George over the poshness of his voice, little knowing his family background. But while George wasn't to the manor born, his wife, Judy, was *seriously* posh. I used to do impressions of her. On one occasion she met Terry Doran, the guy who had the car company with Brian Epstein, and the first thing he said was, 'You're not as good as Tony's impression of you.'

When I went in for the interview, I met two wonderful girls who worked there, Shirley and Carol. I remember Shirley bringing me a cup of tea during the interview, and she was definitely ogling me. *He's nice*, her look seemed to be saying. Shirley was George's long-time personal assistant, and she had this very distinctive, husky, Fenella Fielding-type voice. She looked after George and Ron, while Carol took care of Peter and John. The two women were a great double act: Shirley would come out with all sorts of over-the-top, theatrical remarks, which Carol would undercut with her dose of reality. The pair of them helped make the office sing. They were kind and generous: when Elton first started hanging around, they used to give him their luncheon vouchers. Years later, after George Martin's memorial service, Elton, his partner David Furnish and I took them out to Scott's for lunch.

'You know, I have never really thanked you for all the support you gave me all those years ago,' Elton said.

'And the luncheon vouchers,' Carol immediately chipped in.

To begin with, there wasn't enough room in AIR's Baker Street premises, so I got a desk in Dick James's office instead. Dick, who ran Dick James Music, or DJM, was the publisher of all the Beatles' music. One of the other writing teams he looked after was Hammond Hazlewood. Hammond was Albert Hammond, whose son, Albert Hammond Jr, later became a member of the Strokes; Hazlewood was Mike Hazlewood, whom I subsequently went to live with in America. Among their songs was 'The Air That I Breathe', a huge hit for the Hollies in the early 1970s.

Dick was a great guy, lovely and avuncular, as I mentioned earlier. His secretary, Sue, was married to Ron Harris, who was the captain of Chelsea, and who was also known as 'Chopper' Harris thanks to his reputation as a fierce tackler. At our Christmas parties, a whole host of Chelsea footballers would come along and celebrate with us.

It was because I worked for AIR that I was able to get Elton – or Reg, as he was at the time – some session work with Ron Richards. There was a songwriter called Jerry Lordan, who wrote 'Apache', a huge hit back in the day for the Shadows. He had a new song he wanted to demo, and I asked Reg if he could play on the demo. He played the keyboard part, but then asked about the singing, too. Jerry couldn't hit all the high notes; did I want him to sing as well? At this point, I didn't know he could sing, but I said, 'Why not?' The next day, I took the demo over to AIR, and they all asked who was doing the singing. I explained it was Reg. Ron nodded and said he liked the singing but loved the keyboard-playing.

'Do you think you could get Reg to come along to Abbey Road this afternoon?' he asked. 'I've got a Barron Knights session and I need a keyboard player.'

I called Reg up at home. His mum answered the phone, so I explained who I was and that Reg was wanted up at Abbey Road. 'He'll be paid,' I said. 'Nine quid.'

'He's just cleaning the car,' Reg's mum said, all deadpan. 'I'll ask.'

Reg went up and did the session. Ron was so impressed that he asked him back, this time for a session with the Hollies. One of the songs they were working on was 'He Ain't Heavy, He's My Brother'. Reg played piano on that, and the song became a huge hit.

Reg and I became good friends incredibly quickly. He would often hang out in the office with us. After about a year, I moved to Park Street, where I shared an office with Chris Thomas, who started out as an assistant producer to George, before going on to become an amazing producer in his own right, working with everyone from Roxy Music to Pink Floyd to the Sex Pistols. Reg would come over, and that's where he got to know Shirley and Carol. One year, he came along to the AIR Christmas party, and I did a duet with him – 'I Left my Heart in San Francisco', which I sang in a cod nightclub singer's voice.

Chris Thomas and I both really liked Reg, and we tried different things out for him. We put together a studio band that featured Reg, Bernie Calvert from the Hollies on bass, Caleb Quaye on bass and Roger Pope on drums, and did a session at Abbey Road, co-produced by Chris, where they played songs like 'Mellow Yellow' and 'If I Were a Carpenter'. They went under the name of the Bread and Beer Band. The sessions were fun and the music had a kick to it, but it never went anywhere. The record that resulted from those sessions is now one of those rarities that is worth a fortune if you can find a copy.

Instead, Reg became Elton and released his first album, *Empty Sky*. There's a song on that, 'Skyline Pigeon', that was the first Elton song I really loved: a wonderful, sad ballad that encapsulated his métier. Roger Cooke recorded a version of it, and I plugged the hell out of it. The song didn't quite become a hit, but it received a huge amount of airplay on the BBC. It was just a hint of what was to come. Elton didn't know it – none of us did – but with his next album he would become hugely, properly successful.

———

Throughout the 1960s, I had glimpses into the Beatles and their lives. I had watched from the sidelines during those early, crazy tours, when I was looking after Chris Montez and Roy Orbison. I was there at the party with the Ronettes on the night before the Beatles flew to America for the first time. And I was often a weekend guest at George Harrison's, when he was going out with Pattie. George's house in Esher was a bungalow. It was nice and posh, as far as bungalows went, with a lovely bit of land around it, especially compared to what you got as you moved closer to London.

One of the turning points for the Beatles, I think, was when they first came into contact with the Maharishi Mahesh Yogi. The Maharishi is often credited with the growth and popularisation of Transcendental Meditation, and the Beatles were one of many bands to be influenced by his teachings. In early 1968, they went to Rishikesh, in India, to deepen their understanding of his practices.

The year before, in August 1967, the Maharishi had come to London to give a talk at the Hilton hotel. Pattie and George had first become interested in Eastern philosophy when they travelled to India in 1966. I think Pattie had then been to another lecture on Transcendental Meditation, where she'd been given her mantra. With the exception of Ringo, whose partner Maureen had just given birth to their second child, all the Beatles attended the event at the Hilton, and I went along, too.

The interest in the Maharishi and Eastern philosophy chimed with how 1960s culture was developing. After the dominance of dope as the drug of choice, everybody was now dropping acid, reading *The Tibetan Book of the Dead* and following Timothy Leary. This was the going-to-San-Francisco-and-wearing-flowers-in-your-hair period, and bands started dressing accordingly: lots of bells and kaftans and feathers and what have you. It was the summer of 'All You Need Is Love', and peace and love were in the air.

At the time, it felt quite profound. This was life. But looking back now, it was more of a passing fad, a trend rather than people truly absorbing the cultural meaning behind these things. The Hilton was absolutely packed for the Maharishi's appearance. The man himself sat cross-legged on the stage and talked away. For lots of people there, it was a life-changing experience, but when I left I was merely intrigued. Right from the start I had my reservations about the Maharishi: for all his flowing robes and the long white beard, there always seemed something of the con man to him. In the terminology of the time, I didn't drink the Kool-Aid, though I did sip it. After the talk, I went to the Maharishi Centre in Belgrave Square to get my mantra. Years later, I found it written on the coat hangers in a hotel I was staying at in Sweden, which seemed to sum up the whole experience.

For the Beatles, it turned out to be a tumultuous few weeks. Following the talk, they went to Bangor for a ten-day retreat with the Maharishi. It was while they were there that news came through of the death of their manager, Brian Epstein. I remember being really saddened by his passing. Whenever I'd had dealings with him, Brian had always been an absolute gentleman. He came from a posh Liverpool family who owned a record store in the city. At the beginning of the Beatles' rise to fame, people would come in and ask for records by the band, which was how he first found out about them. Brian was charming. He was calm and never lost his temper. He was very easy to get along with and modest about his achievements, despite the fact that he was managing the biggest band in the world. He always spoke in a very measured way and was never flashy or show-offy in the slightest. I thought that he died of loneliness, in a way, which is a terrible way to go. You can see in the newsreels how stunned John, in particular, was at his death. Cilla was really upset too: Brian was her manager as well, and had taken her from being a hat-check girl in the Cavern to being a big star with her own TV series. She was heartbroken at the news.

The death of Brian and the discovery of Eastern philosophy weren't the only changes for the Beatles in this period. From a musical perspective, the big shift was from being a band that played live to one focused on the studio. Their final concert – the later, short gig on the rooftop of Apple Studios excepted – was at San Francisco's Candlestick Park in August 1966. No longer playing live accelerated the changes in the music they were writing and the way they were recording.

If you're in the thick of it, I'm sure that process is hugely exciting. Personally, I've always found that if you're not directly involved, studios are quite tedious places to be around – endless hanging about and testing the microphones. I always felt a bit like an intruder in someone else's workplace, so I only went down to Abbey Road to see them record occasionally during this period. I did drop in for some of the *Sgt Pepper* sessions. I remember watching them record 'Lovely Rita'. George Martin had an amazing ear for sounds and was very creative musically, too. He turned to me and asked if I could find him combs and some tissue paper – not always the easiest things to find in a recording studio – but I rustled some up, and you can hear the result in the final recording: that strange *whoop, whoop* noise in the background.

Later, I also went to some of the *White Album* recordings. George Martin had gone off on holiday and trusted Chris Thomas enough to take over while he was away. So I watched 'Happiness Is a Warm Gun' unfold and then 'Birthday' being recorded, with Yoko and Pattie on backing vocals. That was a fun session to be at.

My visits, though, were few and far between. As I wasn't in the studio much, I wasn't around often enough to observe how the band's relationships were changing. Some of those changes were inevitable: as the four of them were getting older, they were enjoying different relationships and hanging out with different people. But despite that, when they were together, you could still feel that closeness between them.

People sometimes ask me if the atmosphere changed once Yoko arrived on the scene. I wasn't really around enough to judge, but on reflection I think that the answer has to be yes, that just to have someone in that position, permanently attached to one of the band's main creative forces, was bound to have an effect, to change the dynamics. Paul's wife Linda wasn't there in that way; neither were Pattie or Maureen. And Yoko, being the kind of person she was, was a real presence. She's actually an amazing, extraordinary individual, as I'll explain later, but I didn't really get to know her

85

very well at all during this period. It wasn't until I moved to the States in the 1970s that I got to discover what she was really like.

People change as they get older. Those early weekends when I went to stay with George and Pattie in Esher always felt everyday and fun. After the Maharishi, things felt a little different, a bit less relaxed, a bit more serious, but whether that was a result of how things were changing with the times, how people were changing or how I was changing, I don't know. But when the Beatles did split up, it wasn't a particular surprise to those of us around them, and as seismic as the news might have been for the wider world, my own mind – and heart – was elsewhere.

———

I was in Cannes when I first clapped eyes on Curt. I was there to meet up with Sture Borgedahl, a music publisher whom AIR worked with. I'd been to Sweden previously to see Sture, and we'd got on well. He was a great guy. Every January, there was the Midem Festival in Cannes, which Sture would go to, and so it was suggested that I went along as well, to continue the relationship. I wasn't going to say no to a spot of winter sunshine on the Riviera.

I'd arranged to meet Sture for lunch on the Croisette. La Croisette is a beautiful promenade along the Cannes seafront, lined with hotels, restaurants, casinos and palm trees, with views across the sand out to sea, the blue of the cloudless sky matching that of the Mediterranean below. I walked from where I was staying along the seafront and could see that Sture was sat at the table with someone else. As I came closer, my heart gave a little leap. The man Sture was with had dark hair, a moustache, beautiful eyes and a wonderful smile. As he shook my hand, he held my gaze.

'I'm Curt,' he grinned.

It was what the French would call a *coup de foudre*: instant and unexpected. Sture explained that Curt was a record producer from Sweden, and although we ate and chatted, I found it all but impossible to concentrate on the food or the conversation. My body was consumed by this immediate connection with Curt: it felt so strong and real, extraordinary. I kept on stealing glances at him, wondering if he was feeling the same way.

After lunch, Sture had another meeting to go to, so he said his goodbyes and left Curt and me alone. He was in as much of a daze as I was, and we stumbled back to his hotel, blinking in the bright winter sunshine. We got onto his bed together. We didn't have sex but instead just lay there, looking at each other.

'I don't know what to say,' I said.

Curt stared back at me with his beautiful eyes. 'You have already said it,' he replied.

I'll always remember him saying that and the way he looked at me. 'Oh,' I replied. Then I asked him, 'Do you think it is possible to fall in love this quickly?'

It seemed crazy. I'd met Curt only a couple of hours earlier, yet I was overwhelmed by how I was feeling. And the fact that he was feeling the same way – it was almost too much to hope for. But there it was. We fell in love, instantly, headlong.

When the festival was over, Curt went back to Sweden, and I went back to London. It became a literary affair; we wrote letters and sent telegrams to each other. We arranged for me to go and see him in Sweden, and I was so thrilled, counting down the days to my departure. When I saw him again, my heart soared. And it soared again when he said, 'I want you to come and live with me in Sweden.' He gave me a wedding ring. He had bought one for himself, too, and we had our signatures engraved on the inside of the bands.

My whole world was turned on its head. I'd worked in the music business for over a decade, but Curt was offering me something new and different: a fresh start in another country, a chance to be together. I went back to London and told Ron Richards. I said, 'I think I might be moving to Scandinavia.' I started researching about moving to Sweden and the practicalities of going.

The telegrams continued. And then one day, they stopped. A telegram didn't arrive that day. Or the next. Or the one after that. Overnight, all communication with Curt ceased. I didn't know what to do. I was so frightened that I didn't pick up the phone and call him, as I was so afraid about what he might say. I couldn't sleep. I got terrible insomnia, lying awake night after night, my mind racing. I became really upset and deeply, properly unhappy. I thought we were going to be together, that I'd found the person I was going to spend the rest of my life with. And out of nowhere, he'd dropped me without a word or an explanation. None of it made any sense.

I couldn't work. I was so unhappy that I couldn't concentrate. I had to go to George and say, 'I'm so sorry, I think I'm going to have to leave.' And so I left AIR, and I left London. I didn't want to be around anyone. All the fun and parties of the record industry, I just wasn't in the mood for that any more. I found myself a flat in Lewes, on the south coast, and moved out of London.

Lewes might not have been that far from London, but in terms of atmosphere it was a million miles away. It was so quiet. I lived on the high street, and by six in the evening, the place had cleared out. It was silent – there was no one around. And there was no one I really knew. I made friends with my neighbours, Penny and Graham, who ran a wig shop next door. They became life-long good friends, but most of the time I just kept myself to myself.

It was the most miserable winter. Cold, lonely, sad. Both Charlie Watts and Ringo invited me to New Year's parties they were hosting, and I planned on going, but I came down with flu and couldn't go to either of them. I saw in the New Year feeling terrible and aching all over.

Elton wrote me the most beautiful letter, which I still have. 'Come back, Tone,' he wrote. 'Come back to London. We miss you.' I cried when I read that. Elton explained how Dick James had given him six thousand pounds for his next album, the one with 'Your Song' on it, and it looked like he was finally going to make it. I was so happy for him, and so sad for myself. I knew that this moment, these feelings, would pass, but that winter, in the dark and cold, they felt never-ending.

People were kind to me. That March, AIR London paid for me to go to Scandinavia to see Sture, as a sort of belated leaving present. We went skiing, and I was hoping above hope that I would see Curt there. But he didn't appear. It was lovely to see Sture and great to go skiing, but something was still missing.

Afterwards, we went back to Stockholm. And, finally, I saw Curt. He asked me if I'd stay on a few days, as he'd like to spend some time with me. My heart soared briefly, but from the way he looked at me, or rather didn't, I knew we weren't going to get back together. But at least as we talked I was able to make sense of what had happened. His friends, I think, had talked him out of being with me. They'd spoken to him about the difficulties of bringing someone over to live in Sweden. They said it would be too difficult, too complicated, too disruptive. They influenced him and persuaded him to end the relationship. It was a painful week, not least because Curt was careful to keep his distance. He let me stay in his flat but moved out and stayed somewhere else. He didn't want to have any physical contact with me.

Years later, I was in Stockholm with the Rolling Stones, where they were doing a gig, and I decided to look Curt up. I found out that he had lost his job and had been through some dark times himself. He was now working in a tourist office, giving advice about what to do and see in Stockholm.

I went in to see him. 'Hello,' I said.

He looked at me oddly for a moment, then realised who I was. 'Oh, hello,' he said. 'How are you?'

'I'm fine.' I explained what I was doing there, and why I was in town. 'I wondered if we could meet for lunch, or for coffee at least?'

Curt agreed to meet up in a cafe, and we just talked.

'It was strange what happened between us,' I said.

Curt nodded and said, 'Yes.'

'You know, I really loved you, Curt.' I could feel a lump in my throat. 'And I think I always will, in a special way.'

Curt nodded. 'Yes,' he agreed. 'What we had was something very special.'

That was the last time I saw him. Years later, I went to the memorial for Sture Borgedahl in London. After the service, I caught up with Marcus Österdahl, a music arranger. Marcus, I knew, had been very friendly with Curt, so I asked him how he was.

'I'm so sorry,' he said, 'but he died of cancer.'

Love, it turns out, isn't always all you need.

7

Although my relationship with Curt was over, at least that final trip to Sweden unlocked something for me. When I got back to England, I was ready to work again, ready to leave Lewes, move back to London and start over.

Unfortunately, it took a while for a proper job to open up. To begin with, the only position I could find was answering the telephones at one of the large HMV record shops, which I had to take just to make ends meet. Elton used to ring up and tease me. He'd put on a fake voice and ask me to run around the store and look for this or that record for him. It was only when I got back and heard him laughing that I'd realise who it was. 'You bugger,' I'd growl down the phone at him.

Then I got the offer of a job working for Pye Records, doing promotion under Johnny Wise, whom I got on with, and who liked me a lot. There was another person who worked there called Peter Prince, who was a friend of mine and Charlie Watts. It was a good atmosphere and it helped me get back into the swing of things. I wasn't there for that long, but I worked on 'In the Summertime' by Mungo Jerry and 'Lola' by the Kinks, both of which turned out to be huge hits. When I left there after a couple of months, everyone was disappointed.

'But we were just getting to know you,' I remember one person saying.

I felt the same, but an opportunity had come up that was too good to turn down.

The first time I was offered a job by Apple, I turned them down. To begin with, I could see how chaotic the organisation was, with all these people floating around like hippies and nothing getting done. I thought I was better off carrying on working with George Martin, whose outfit was far more professional, so I stayed put. By the time I decided to join Apple, the situation had changed. The Beatles had split, and Allen Klein had come in and taken over the company. The set-up was much slicker, and Apple was beginning to go places. And so this time I said yes.

Allen Klein was someone whom I always had a lot of time for. I know that for some music fans he can be a bit of a divisive figure, but I was never involved with him on the business side of things – royalties, contracts, that sort of thing. It's probably fair to say that he was a wheeler and a dealer, but I never got on the wrong side of him. He was always fair with me, and we got on really well.

He was razor sharp, business-wise, but there was more to him than just that. He was musically on the money as well and could talk in great detail and with real knowledge about John Lennon's career from a creative standpoint, as well as just the business side of things. That was one of the reasons I always really liked him. He truly understood music and musicians. I'd seen at first hand how he had supported Andrew Loog Oldham when he was managing the Stones. Later, when I was living in New York, I'd go to dinner with Allen and his partner Iris, and they'd always be warm, relaxed evenings.

That kindness towards me continued with his children. When I was later working for the Stones again and we did the *Forty Licks* project, we got Pharrell Williams to do a remix of 'Sympathy for the Devil'. Jody, Allen's son, supervised that, and he came out to see the band in Hungary, where they were touring. He set up a listening room in the hotel so that the band could come and listen to the remix. They were hugely appreciative and thought highly of him. Allen's daughter Robyn is the same. She wrote to me recently and said, 'My father always loved you.' So I'm always going to be kind about Allen!

Apple was a great place to work. The office on Savile Row had a warm vibe, a tone that was set by Ringo, who was often around. Everyone likes Ringo – he is a simple, honest man. There is never any bullshit with him, and that seemed to permeate through the building. It started at reception. Laurie, the switchboard operator, had a wonderfully seductive voice: 'Apple, good morning!' And the relaxed, seductive atmosphere spread to everyone who worked there.

Among other things, I was head of A&R, which meant that all and sundry would turn up to see me, trying to convince me to sign them up as the next big thing. Many of them were just trying: I always remember a woman, her breasts all but hanging out, singing 'Sometimes I Feel Like a Motherless Child'. I got all sorts of eccentrics. One day a guy appeared, telling me he was God. The next day, completely separately, a French man turned up claiming to be Jesus Christ.

'That's funny,' I told him. 'I had your father in yesterday.'

Lots of people were always coming and going. Elton used to drop in to see me, which everyone used to love; Margo, my secretary, would fuss over him and make him a cup of tea whenever he appeared. I got Elton's nephew Paul a job as an office boy. He was lovely. All the office boys were lovely, in fact. It felt like family, which is how the best offices should feel. Keith Moon, the Who's drummer, would come in to see Ringo. We had an Apple darts team, and Keith used to play for that sometimes. One time, I remember he was so drunk during a match that he couldn't stand up straight. The office boys had to hold him up so he wasn't horizontal and could at least try to aim at the board. Marc Bolan was another star who used to drop by – again, to see Ringo. He was very fey and had this wonderful wife, June, whom Elton and I adored. She was very well-to-do and extremely funny.

Someone else who would drop in and see me was Kenny Everett, which would always go down well. I originally met Kenny through another friend of mine, Don Paul, who was originally in a group called the Viscounts. He was having a fling with Kenny, and I was introduced to him. We immediately hit it off. Kenny was a bit unsure about his sexuality at this point and ended up marrying another friend of mine, a woman called Lee. She used to live with Billy Fury, and I often went down to their house in Surrey for the weekend – in fact, I remember I was staying there when the Stones got busted for drugs. We all crowded round the television and watched as the news came in. Lee and Billy broke up, and then Lee went out with Kenny. Kenny decided that she was going to be his salvation, and so he proposed to her.

Kenny and Lee's wedding was something else. I hired them a horse-drawn carriage, complete with a pair of beautiful dray horses, to take us up Kensington High Street to the registry office. Lee had a wedding dress made out of a tablecloth she had bought in Harrods, as she couldn't find a dress she liked. For reasons I can't remember, it was decided to have the reception before the wedding. It was catered for by two stunning transexuals, Pat and Lorraine, and we all got plastered on Pimm's. Lee's mother was so drunk that she had to be held up by security guards for the service. After the wedding, when we got back to Kenny's flat, there was a second Pimm's punch, which had a distinctly different colour to the first. I took one look at it and instinct told me to steer well clear. This turned out to be the right choice: the punch was spiked with amphetamines, and when Lee and Kenny went off on their honeymoon, they were awake all through the first night, unable to get to sleep.

Kenny and Lee bought a house together in Sussex called Cowfold. I used to drive over from Lewes to their place on a Saturday night, and we'd head to his studio, put the headphones on, smoke a lot of dope and listen to music. *Music of My Mind* by Stevie Wonder was one album we'd listen to that sounded amazing. 'Goodbye to Love' by the Carpenters, with the guitar playout at the end, was another that always did it for me. I'd get too stoned to drive back and would end up staying over. Kenny had a pair of friends called Franz and Pots – two crazy, mad queens, one German, the other from northern England – and they would often be there as well. It was always great fun.

Kenny was very mischievous. There was one occasion when I was staying in London with Mafalda, who by this point was no longer with Tony Hall. The apartment was in Porter Street, and I was renting a room for a short while. A couple of people were over and there were a lot of high spirits, and before I knew it I had agreed to streak for a dare. I took off my clothes and went down to the door on Porter Street, then ran full pelt along Baker Street, right past McDonald's, where a woman in the window, about to eat, just stared in amazement. Afterwards, I wasn't all that keen on telling people what had taken place, but I quietly told Kenny the story, and he took it upon himself to mention it on his radio show, so suddenly everyone I knew was aware of what I'd done.

———

There was a real sense of creativity at Apple in those years. There were a load of new and exciting artists the label was releasing,

Badfinger and Mary Hopkin among them. John, Paul, George and Ringo all seemed to thrive on separating and doing their own stuff.

I worked on the promotion of George's first solo album, *All Things Must Pass*. That is an amazing album, and I can't quite believe it is now over fifty years old. Phil Spector's production is incredible and a huge part of the reason why the album was such a success. It was such a grand record, tremendously elegant, with this huge sense of sweep.

It was lovely, too, to see (and help) George step out of the shadows. He'd always written great music – 'Something', for example, is just wonderful – but his songs had always appeared only sporadically on the Beatles' albums and he was very much in the back seat. Finally, he had space to show what he could do, and he delivered in spades. He was never boastful about the album's success, but I knew he was quietly satisfied with how it did. The packaging of the album was also fantastic. I love that picture of him sitting in Friar Park with all the gnomes – that wonderful guru look he had, with the beard and everything. Even the title works so well – that nod to the fact that the Beatles' time was over, and now here he was, finally able to be himself.

John, too, was firing on all cylinders. I was brought in to do some work on 'Cold Turkey' and 'Power to the People'. I remember Allen Klein calling me into a meeting to talk about the latter with John and Yoko. That was the first time I'd met Yoko properly and I was a bit wary of her, just because of some of the stuff I'd heard. But she just sat there, very still, very enigmatic. John did all the talking.

The album I had the biggest involvement with was *Ringo*, Ringo's third and most successful solo record. His popularity in the music business was made clear by the sheer number of guest stars who featured on it. As well as contributions from the other three Beatles, Marc Bolan, Klaus Voormann, Steve Cropper, Robbie Robertson, Martha Reeves and Harry Nilsson were among those who were involved. Everyone wanted it to be a success. I was given the job of pulling together all the disparate elements for the record, which was no easy task – sorting out the cover, dealing with the producers, chasing them up on the mixes, organising the artwork, photographs and drawings. It was a job that combined the various skills I'd learned over the years: progress chaser, project manager, promoter and people person – building those relationships and getting things out of people on time.

Ringo had this very eccentric guy who looked after him called Hilary Gerrard. I would often walk upstairs to Ringo's office to talk to Hilary. I would go in, but though I could hear his voice, I couldn't see him. Then I'd notice the telephone wire working its way down under his desk, where Hilary was sat. 'I'm under the desk today,' he'd say. 'I can't cope.'

Hilary had a bearded wild-man-of-the-woods look to him. He had a flat opposite Lord's cricket ground with filthy windows, apart from a circular hole he'd cleaned in them so he could watch the cricket through a telescope. He had a wonderful, long, beautifully manicured cocaine fingernail, on which he would offer you coke. Ringo was very fond of him.

After the album came out, we went to Mexico to do some promotion. I remember they gave us a couple of days' holiday in Las Brisas hotel, in Acapulco. It's a strange place, pink all over. And by that, I mean everything in the hotel was pink – the pool, the towels, the paint. Wherever you looked, it was pink. It was fun at first, but after a couple of days, you never again wanted to see anything pink in your life.

In 1972, I asked Allen Klein if I could go to America.

'Why?' he asked.

'Because it is the soundtrack of my life,' I explained. 'Everything that I have ever loved is American. American music, American movies, I just feel I have to go there and experience it.'

And Allen said, 'That's as good a reason as I've ever heard.'

So I flew out to the US for the first time with Ringo and George Harrison, when they went to accept an award for the Bangladesh concert. Visiting New York City felt like someone had just plugged me into the mains. 'The First Time Ever I Saw Your Face' by Roberta Flack was number one. 'Layla' was a big hit, too. I listened to that while smoking a joint in a taxi driving down Broadway. The bit where it segues into the second half of the song, with the city spinning past, made it feel like I was in seventh heaven.

Everything about the city felt sensuous. The people, the atmosphere. The first night, Ringo and I went downtown to an Italian restaurant with one of Allen Klein's people. The place had great food, but I remember it also had this amazing jukebox. The woman who served us had a black beehive and pink lipstick, the jukebox was playing 'My Prayer' by the Platters, and I was thinking, *Oh my God, this is almost like someone has laid on a soundtrack for me, because it is so brilliant.*

Sixteen years after I first heard 'Heartbreak Hotel' in my childhood home in Eastbourne, I also got see my idol. Elvis was playing a series of four concerts at Madison Square Garden, and George asked if I'd like to go with him and Pattie.

'Would I ever!' was my reply.

The 1972 Elvis was very much in his cape period. It was amazing to see him in the flesh, but disappointing at the same time: it wasn't the young, hip-swinging 1950s version I had in my head. Mind you, it wasn't the later bloated-period Elvis either, so I should be grateful for that. And he did play 'Heartbreak Hotel'.

In the intermission, one of Elvis's team appeared and asked George if he'd like to go backstage and meet the man himself. George disappeared with this guy, leaving me regretting not asking if I could come, too. After a while, just before the second half of the show began, George reappeared.

'Well?' I asked. 'How was he?'

George shrugged. 'He was all right, I guess. He didn't say much.'

The lights went down. And that was as close as I ever got to meeting Elvis.

———

New York was a sexy city. The people on the street were sexy. Everybody looked like they were cruising. I got the impression everyone, male and female, was looking for a bit of an adventure. Compared to London, it had an energy and a vibe.

Nowhere was this truer than in the two cities' contrasting gay life. On that first trip to New York, I took the time to go to the Continental Baths, and it was like stepping into a different world. They had a dance floor, a hairdressing salon, a gym. The Baths were where Bette Midler was originally discovered. She did cabaret there (with Barry Manilow conducting, I believe), and the men would sit around in towels, listening to her perform.

I took a look around and thought, *This is fabulous, but where is the action?* Then I saw people going off into a room. Each time they opened the door, puffs of steam would come out. I followed them in, but as soon as I entered the room, I realised it was pitch black. I froze and stood against the wall, thinking, *This is* way *too dangerous.* I left and loitered outside again, watching more rather handsome people go back in.

Fuck it, I thought, *I've got to just do it.* So I went back in and stood against the wall until my eyes adjusted for the light. At this point, I realised it was laid out like a maze. As I walked down, I could see the maze was punctuated by niches and nooks, and in each of these there were people having sex. I had got halfway down, when a hand reached out from one of the niches and pulled me in, and I joined four other people. When I came out the other side, I felt like I had been through a washer–dryer! It was a fantastic experience, and it was one that changed me. I felt liberated. That this was all OK gave me a sense of freedom.

After this first trip, I just couldn't wait to go back. London, by comparison, seemed a bit stale. The *Ringo* album allowed me a second bite, and I returned, this time to Los Angeles, to help pull the album together. Apple Capitol – Ringo's American label – didn't want someone from Apple UK embedded there, but someone else had other ideas. While I was in LA, I ended up in the Roxy with John Lennon one night. He leaned across the table and said, 'I want you to work for me in America.'

I protested at first. 'I'm not so sure,' I said. 'I've got a home and a life in London.'

'Come on,' John replied, 'what do you want to live in Denmark for?' When I looked confused, he said, 'England's like Denmark – it's so boring.' He was insistent, and in the end, I agreed.

To work in the States, I needed a visa. And to get a visa, I needed the approval of every Beatle. By the early 1970s, getting the signature of all four on anything was fraught with band politics. Getting the approval of John, Ringo and George was OK; the process of getting Paul's signature was more difficult. I went to see him; he was rehearsing with Wings at the time.

'This is my future, Paul,' I explained. 'I really need this.'

Paul understood, but explained that because he was in dispute with the other three, he couldn't sign anything. I felt deflated, but then Paul offered a possible solution. If his lawyer signed, would that work? I went back and, thankfully, that was accepted.

———

I set off for America in style. When I told Elton what I was doing, he said that he was heading for New York as well.

'I'm going by boat,' he said. 'On the SS *France*. Do you want to join us?'

Elton was travelling with his band. John Lennon wanted to see his son, so I took Julian and John's ex-wife Cynthia along with me. Before we set off, I imagined that the cruise would be like something from a Fred Astaire and Ginger Rogers movie, all dinner parties, glamour and shiny dance floors. In reality, it turned out to be anything but. All the flower vases were mag-netised so they wouldn't fall over. You had to give them a really good tug to shift them. Elton and I used to amuse ourselves by asking people to bring a vase over, then giggle as they struggled to move it.

The weather was terrible. Not that there's much to see in the middle of the Atlantic anyway, but there was fog for the entire five-day trip. So all the fun was inside. Elton and I played squash together – badly. We also played bingo. I remember Elton winning seventeen pounds and saying, 'I'm keeping my winnings.' In the evening, the cabaret consisted of a French singer doing an Édith Piaf-style set in a Lurex shirt, two Russian singers who belted out 'Hava Nagila', a magician and a German opera singer who made everyone's ears hurt.

When we weren't messing about together, Elton was writing songs for *Captain Fantastic and the Brown Dirt Cowboy*. He booked a room to rehearse in, which he had to share with an opera singer, each of them having two hours at a time. There was no tape recorder or anything to make notes with, so he had to remember all the songs in his head.

Not everyone was impressed by our presence. One wealthy woman loudly and dismissively said, 'That man over there is Elton John – he is very famous, apparently, but I have never heard of him.'

When we arrived in New York, the record company had sent over a fleet of limos to pick us all up. We were ushered off the boat ahead of everybody else, and I remember looking back at the woman and thinking, *Fuck you, missus.*

8

Trying to reverse-park a Thunderbird is not the easiest manoeuvre at the best of times. But in the packed restaurant car park in Santa Monica, it felt more difficult than it should have done. That was down to my passenger, John Lennon, who with his familiar round glasses and short hair was sniggering and chuckling at my attempts to squeeze the car into a space. Flustered at the fact I'd got the angles all wrong again, I lined the car up once more and prepared to have another go.

My time in Los Angeles working on pulling together Ringo Starr's album had been coming to an end when I got the call. It was May Pang, who at the time I thought was John's assistant.

'John and I are coming to LA tomorrow,' May said, 'and he wondered whether we could meet?'

May said that they were staying at Havenhurst, which as it happened was just around the corner from where I was, on Fountain, where I'd been living with songwriter Mike Hazlewood, whom I'd known since my time working at AIR.

'Do you think you could pick us up around seven-thirty?' May asked.

As I drove over, I remember feeling a bit nervous. I'd come across John on and off ever since the early days of the Beatles, and I knew how sharp-tongued he could be. He was more than capable of putting you in your place if he wanted to. He could be quite cutting.

But John was special, too. I always say that, of the Beatles, he was the José Mourinho – the special one. He was the one everyone wanted to know. And for all the sharpness of his tongue, there was also the plaintive tone of his voice. When I watched the band sing 'All You Need Is Love' at the live TV recording, there was something about the way he sang the opening lines that cuts through beautifully. It's to do with the tremor.

So when I pulled up and I saw him standing there – if you'll forgive the pun – I was made up at how pleased he seemed to be to see me. He was smiling away and gave me a hug. I was delighted, but also thinking, *Why are you making such a fuss of me?* He and May climbed into the Thunderbird, and I drove to the restaurant.

Even though John couldn't have been nicer, there was something about him being in the car that was intimidating. It was a particularly hot LA day, and I could feel my hands starting to sweat against the steering wheel. When we got to the restaurant car park, I gulped at how busy it was. Thunderbirds are big cars to swing around, and there was something about John's presence that was putting me off.

'What's wrong?' John asked, laughing.

'What's wrong,' I said, crunching through the gears, 'is you being in the car with me.'

The more flustered I got, the funnier John found it. And the funnier John found it, the more flustered I became.

'Well, what are you going to suggest then?' John asked.

'I am going to suggest that you get out of the car, go into the restaurant and get the table in my name.' I gave John a look. 'And I will come in when I have parked the car.'

So he and May got out, and I sat there watching until they'd gone in and I knew they were no longer looking at me. In an instant, I relaxed. I put the car into reverse and swerved it into the space.

By the time I joined John and May at the table, they were roaring with laughter. John thought it was hilarious that I'd ordered him out of the car and made him go and wait in the restaurant. It might not sound like much, but from that moment of humour, it felt as though we really began to communicate. And although the meal was a business one – John had been impressed with what I'd done for Ringo's album and wanted me to come and work for him – we struck up a friendship as well. We became really close throughout the time that I worked for him.

———

John was with Cynthia when I first met him. I remembered her being very attentive towards him at Tony Hall's party, before the Beatles went to the States for the first time. And I remembered him and Yoko together when I was at Apple.

But it was only now, in Los Angeles, that I felt I got to know him properly. At the restaurant, we ended up talking about our families, our mothers, our upbringings and life in general. It was one of those deep, soulful conversations, and then John explained to me how he had split from Yoko. The way he explained it, I got the impression that it wasn't going to be for ever. She had asked him to leave because he had been unfaithful to her at a party in New York at which she'd been present. Yoko had wanted him to leave her, and yet she'd wanted him to leave with May. Essentially, she had set May up as his girlfriend, and then would call up every day to check in on him. I knew she was always there in the background.

John was very keen for me to meet Yoko. He was insistent, in fact. She came out to California to do a performance in San Diego with her band, so I went to watch. Afterwards, she was lovely with me. 'You always do nice things for me with Apple,' she told me. She was very approving of the ads that I put together for her whenever an album or single came out. I remember one song called 'Mind Train', where I worked up a picture with her face in negative. She really liked that.

On another occasion, I had to go to New York, and John asked me to go and see her. 'She is a great lady,' he told me. I remember that quite distinctly: 'a great lady' is what he called her. I rang her up, and she told me to come over to the Dakota building, where their apartment was, and we'd go out for tea. I was quite surprised when she said this. I thought, *This doesn't sound like the imperious person I was expecting.*

When I got to the Dakota and she opened the door, she looked so fragile, like a little bird. We went out, down 72nd Street to a normal, everyday coffee place. On the table where we sat was a silver container full of napkins.

We started to talk, and Yoko asked me, 'So, how is John?'

'He is OK, Yoko,' I said. 'He is fine.'

There was a pause. Then Yoko said simply, 'I miss him so much.' And she began to cry.

I started pulling napkins out of the silver container and passing them across to her.

'Don't get upset,' I said.

But she continued to cry, and I kept on passing her napkins. Eventually, just as I was beginning to worry I was going to run out of them, she stopped. I felt for her, for how vulnerable she was. She was in a difficult position: she wasn't ready to take John back, but she wasn't ready to lose him either. I knew how strong Yoko was, so seeing her like this was difficult, but considering where John was at, she didn't want him back in her life at this point.

May Pang, by contrast, was pretty together. She was always measured and cool, and very attractive, too. She had an amazing figure, beautiful long hair and a lovely way of being around people. She was always smiling and was popular with everyone – a calming presence to have around. She couldn't have been nicer with me, and I found her extremely helpful in my job looking after John. I guess we were both doing that, but he was leaning on us for different sorts of support. In its own way, May's position was as difficult as Yoko's. It must have been a strange situation, to be there as the approved girlfriend. But I never discussed the situation with her. We didn't talk about it and just got on with things.

After I went to see Yoko, I reported back to John. He wanted to know everything that had been said. But otherwise I left their situation alone and watched it play out as I suspected it would. That moment at the Madison Square Garden concert, the look between them, told me everything I needed to know.

———

Although John was the special one of the Beatles, he had been the least successful since the band's split. I think that was one of the reasons why he wanted me to work for him. He had a lawyer who handled the business side of things, but he needed a manager on the creative side, to steer him. John knew what I'd done with Apple, and that's what he wanted me to bring to his own music.

Right at the start of our relationship, he asked me what I thought of his situation. I was straight with him.

'To be honest, John,' I told him, 'you have fallen out of favour with the public because of the politics, and because of some of the people you've been hanging out with.'

Back in New York, John had befriended all sorts of activists. People like Jerry Rubin, a founding member of the Youth

International Party, who undertook 'guerrilla theatre' stunts, such as stopping the New York Stock Exchange by throwing money in the air. He was one of the Chicago Seven, who were charged with conspiracy and incitement to riot after an anti-war demonstration ended in violence, and whose case was later made into a film.

In 1971, John had taken part in a rally protesting against the sentencing of John Sinclair, a poet and activist who had been charged with possession of marijuana and had received a ten-year sentence. John wrote a song named after him, 'John Sinclair', and performed it at the rally. The protests worked, and Sinclair was released, but the result was that John was now on the FBI's radar. Around the same time, US President Richard Nixon drew up an 'Enemies List'. John was in danger of being added to this, and unlike others on it, such as Jane Fonda and Gene Hackman, he had the threat of deportation hanging over him.

I said to John, 'You've got yourself in a position where people think of you as a bit of a leftie, you know.' In America, more so than in the UK, being seen to be on the left was a big deal commercially. In terms of selling records and getting played on the radio, it was a problem. I knew that John was passionate about the causes he was fighting for, and I didn't want to stop him doing that. But I didn't think that his audience, who weren't engaged with the same issues necessarily, had to be alienated at the same time. He just needed some repositioning to bring his fans with him.

'So what do we do?' John asked.

'I think what is needed is for you to do some nice, friendly interviews with the music papers and re-establish yourself again.'

'OK,' said John. 'Set it up.'

My involvement caused a bit of resentment from Capitol, his record label. They'd normally arrange the interviews, but I went off and set them up myself. I organised one with *Record World*, another with *Creem* magazine, and suddenly John was getting all this good press, in a way he hadn't been for years. John was on his best behaviour throughout. When he turned up for the interview with *Creem*, the journalist asked him if he'd like to smoke a joint. John declined, telling me afterwards, 'I am always wary when they offer you that. Because they know they are going to get more out of you.'

The first of John's albums I worked on was *Mind Games*. The campaign for it featured a somewhat unusual TV commercial. The idea came when Mike Hazlewood and I got stoned one night at his house in LA, and for reasons I can't remember I began doing an impersonation of the Queen telling people to go and buy the album. Mike laughed his head off, and then he recorded it. Afterwards, I had an idea.

'Let's play it to John as a surprise,' I said. We carried the tape machine out to the car and put it on the back seat. We picked John up and were driving down Sunset Boulevard, when Mike pressed play on the tape player. Suddenly, there was my impersonation of the Queen booming out. John was hysterical with laughter.

I thought no more about it, but then the next day John rang me up.

'I want to do a TV commercial, with you as the Queen advertising *Mind Games*,' he said.

'OK,' I said, shocked. 'Fine, sure, if that's what you want.'

It got more surreal when I realised I had to find a costume to wear as the Queen. I went down to Western Costume, a store used by Hollywood, but my visit coincided with Halloween. Back then, hardly anyone in the UK bothered with Halloween, and I had no idea how big a deal it was in the US. Rather than being able to slip in and out quietly, the store was packed.

'Which one of you is the Queen?' the woman behind the counter shouted. Everyone turned to look at me as I raised my hand. I must have annoyed the people queuing because I kept on rejecting the dresses they sent out for me to try on.

'No,' I said, turning down yet another. 'Her Majesty wouldn't be seen *dead* in that.'

Eventually, they found one that had enough of a ballgown look to it.

The recording took place at a studio in Santa Monica. Elton was in town, and I'd talked to John about him quite a lot. 'You'd like him,' I'd said. So when I suggested that Elton come along to the recording, John said he'd really like to meet him.

It was quite a weird introduction, as Elton turned up in the middle of my getting changed. I stood there wearing a crown and make-up, but still in my jeans: 'Elton, John . . . John, Elton.'

There was a great atmosphere in the studio. May was there, as were Roy Cicala, who ran the Record Plant studio in New York, and Jimmy Iovine. I sat resplendent on a throne, a bottle of vodka stashed underneath it. The crew were hilarious. One guy, who was particularly attractive, came up to me and said, 'Do you want to fool around, Your Majesty?'

I gave him a regal look and said, 'Later, baby.'

The advert itself opened with 'Land of Hope and Glory' playing and a pair of doors opening to reveal me sat on the throne, sceptre in one hand and a copy of *Mind Games* in the other. 'Good evening,' I said, doing my best impersonation of Her Majesty. 'I have been asked to do this commercial. It relates to a gramophone record called *Mind Games* by John Lennon.' Then the music cut to the title song of the album, and the camera zoomed in on the sleeve.

You can hear John sniggering in the background. In the off-cuts, there's footage of John and me dancing, and of Elton taking Polaroids from behind the cameras.

It was a really fun day. We did a lot of TV spots for the album and loads of press promotion. For John's next album, *Walls and Bridges*, we ran a fantastic billboard campaign. It was common for the advertising campaigns to be farmed out, but I knew that there were a lot of talented people at Capitol, so I made the decision to create this one in house. They were delighted by that and delivered accordingly. We had these amazing ads, with a strip of John's face in the middle and 'Listen To This Ad' across the top. For TV, we copied the idea, but changed the line to 'Listen To This Commercial', with Ringo doing the voiceover. It was a great campaign and convinced me that I should work directly with the record company whenever possible.

———

Two old contacts were to play a big part in my time looking after John. The first of these was the record producer Lou Adler, whom I'd known since working with Andrew Loog Oldham. Andrew and Lou were great friends. Among the artists that Lou had produced were Carole King and the Mamas and the Papas.

One night, John and I were at the Roxy, on Sunset Strip. Above it was another club, On the Rocks, which was run by Lou. Lou came over to say hi, and we started talking. He asked John where he was staying, and John explained that he was living with his lawyer, Harold Seider. Lou had an idea.

'Would you like to stay at my house in Bel Air?' Lou asked. 'I'm living at my house by the beach at the moment, so if you'd like to stay there, it's yours.'

He said 'house', but Lou's Bel Air property was definitely more of a mansion, and John and May duly moved in.

The second old acquaintance who played a big role in this period was another producer, Phil Spector. I write about Spector here as I encountered him then – not, as he later became, the convicted murderer of Lana Clarkson and abuser of multiple women. If my reminiscences seem strangely innocent, it is because the side of the man I got to meet was clearly only a small part of the whole. I'd first come across Phil back when I was looking after the Ronettes. He was always mischievous. He'd hang out with Andrew, and the pair of them together were like naughty schoolboys. They'd wind me up. Phil wouldn't play the publicity game either. Whatever I'd set up for him to do, he'd mess around with.

He'd hassle me for money as well. One time, I was in the promotions office in Hanover Square, when he rang me up. He had this thin, light tone when he spoke, which was instantly recognisable.

'Hey, Tony,' he said. 'I'm in Fenwick's. Do you know Fenwick's?'

'Yes, I know Fenwick's,' I said, a sinking feeling in my stomach.

'I've spent quite a lot of money,' Phil explained. 'Do you think I might be able to get my royalties to pay for it?'

'Let me see what I can do.'

I rang through to Bill Townsley, who was second in command at the label, under Sir Edward Lewis. He had a wonderful secretary, Ann, who was, thankfully, very together.

'We've got a problem,' I explained to her. 'Phil Spector is in Fenwick's, having spent a huge amount of money, and needs his royalties to pay the bill.'

Ann wasn't fazed at all. 'We'll take care of it,' she said.

They advanced the money, and the bill got settled.

Musically, Phil was a genius. Andrew loved how he produced, and he tried to copy him. Phil and I continued to work together, and when I was at Apple I arranged the promotion for his Christmas album. He came and did three days of publicity, and this time there were no issues.

Phil liked and trusted me. Later, when I was on tour working with the Stones, he even asked me to look after his daughter for him. I wasn't afraid to be straight with him. I remember going to the Rock and Roll Hall of Fame in 1988, when the Beatles were inducted by Mick Jagger. Phil was in Allen Klein's suite and was acting up, making all kinds of statements. I told him to pack it in, whereupon I was accosted by one of his bodyguards, a huge guy squeezed into a suit.

'You can't speak to Mr Spector like that,' the bodyguard told me.

'Listen,' I said. 'I've known Mr Spector for a long time and I will say what I want.'

The bodyguard was about three times my size, but he backed off. I turned to Phil. 'Don't be awkward now,' I said. 'Stop being silly.'

And Phil took it: he calmed down, and the moment was defused.

Like I've said, there was obviously a darker side to Phil than that which I saw, one that culminated in his arrest and conviction for Lana Clarkson's murder in 2009. Those later events were a horrific, shocking end and a grim counterpoint to a hugely influential musical career.

———

John had decided that he wanted to record a rock-and-roll album to follow up *Mind Games*, and he wanted Phil Spector to produce it. This was during his 'Lost Weekend', as he referred to the eighteen-month period during which he and Yoko were separated. Away from Yoko, John was letting his hair down. Phil's earlier mischievousness, meanwhile, was becoming tinged with a darker edge, and the recording sessions became more rock-and-roll than the rock and roll the band were recording. Drink and drugs and party guests and hangers-on filled the studio. Warren Beatty, David Geffen, Joni Mitchell and many others would drop by, and it all became quite raucous and riotous.

I went to one of the sessions, when they were recording 'Sweet Little Sixteen'. I'm not a big fan of recording studios, as I've already mentioned, and I didn't feel at all comfortable the entire time I was there. The whole set-up felt borderline out of control; it was all too edgy. John was a little crazy. Phil was a little crazy. And all the musicians involved were drinking like crazy. I made my excuses, as the saying goes, and left. And that wasn't even the worst of it: on another occasion Phil famously pulled out a gun as a prank and fired it in the control room. Mike Hazlewood was one of the musicians involved, and he would give me progress reports. He told me he used to take a bottle of vodka to the sessions in his guitar case. Instinct told me not to get involved in the craziness.

My instincts were proved right when I was woken up at 3 a.m. one morning. It was May Pang on the phone, and she sounded panicked.

'You've got to come to the house,' she said. 'There has been some trouble.'

In the background I could hear shouting and the sound of something being smashed.

'What is that noise?' I asked.

'It's John,' May said. 'Please, Tony. Hurry.'

Shaking myself awake, I got dressed and jumped in my Thunderbird. As I pulled up to the house, I could see May out on the street, waving her arms at me. Behind her, inside, I could hear John shouting.

'What is going on?' I slammed the car door behind me.

May looked as worried as she sounded. 'Everything got crazy at the studio,' she explained. 'Crazier than normal. Everyone had been drinking and doing God knows what. John was a mess, so Phil and his bodyguard brought him back to the house. They tied him up and left him there to calm down. Except John broke free and now he's . . .'

Behind her, I could hear another smash.

'OK.' I handed May the keys. 'Keep the engine running, because if this gets out of hand, I am not hanging around.'

I took a deep breath and starting walking up the driveway. In front of me, I could see a silhouette of John in the doorway, shouting. At first, I wasn't sure what he was doing, but then I realised that he was trying to pull a palm tree out of the ground, without much success. I could see that windows were smashed and, behind him, the gold records for *Tapestry* and *The Mamas and the Papas* that lined the walls had been pulled off and scattered across the floor, where they lay twisted and bent. I didn't even know you could do that to a gold record.

As I walked up, John clocked me. There was a wild look in his eyes. The only thing that I could think to say to him was, 'What is the matter with you? What is going on?' And at that moment, he just seemed to crumple. He broke down, fell on my shoulder and started sobbing. 'They tied me up,' he kept on repeating. 'They tied me up.'

He was clearly shaken by what had happened. And not without reason. The Manson murders had taken place in LA only a few years earlier and were still in the back of everyone's mind. I hugged him and said, 'Come on. Let's go inside and sit down.'

If you're familiar with drinking and how some people who drink have blackouts, then you'll know how they can switch without much notice. That's what happened now. One minute I was helping John in and he seemed to have calmed down, the next he'd turned on me and was starting to fight. We collapsed onto the floor in a heap. For a moment we were rolling back and forth, until finally I was able to clamber on top of him. I lay there, pinning his arms down by his side so he couldn't take a swing at me. Our faces were almost nose to nose.

As quickly as he went into it, John came out of the blackout again. His expression changed from anger to confusion to mirth.

'I never knew you were so strong, dear,' he said, and we both burst out laughing. I pulled him up and sat him down. He had another blackout a few moments later, but again I was able to calm him down. I called May in and told her he was OK, but said I'd stay the night, just to be sure. I slept in one of the rooms with the broken windows.

The following morning, the clean-up began. In the light of day I could see that the floors were covered in glass. The windows could be replaced; the gold records on the wall were a more difficult matter. I got on the phone to Nancy Andrews, who was Lou Adler's assistant (and, later on, Ringo's girlfriend). I explained what had happened and asked her if there was a way we could sort out the damage without Lou knowing. Between us, we somehow managed to get everything fixed and replaced, and it was only much later that Lou found out.

However much he might have drunk that night, John woke the following morning feeling refreshed. We went for a late breakfast with producer Jimmy Iovine and Roy Cicala. The meal was light and full of laughter, as though nothing had ever happened. That was John all over: he had a carefree attitude to life, which was one of the reasons people loved him. And he was kind, too. To say thank you for sorting out the house, he gave me a picture of Marilyn Monroe by Andy Warhol. On the back was a handwritten note: 'To Tony with love, from one of your problems, John.' It remains one of my most treasured possessions.

———

In the middle of John's 'Lost Weekend', we had a wild weekend ourselves: a trip to Las Vegas. John had wanted to go, and it's not an offer you can refuse, is it? He and May caught a flight there, while I drove over from LA with Mike Hazlewood to meet them.

We were booked in at Caesar's Palace hotel, and when I arrived, John told me that Fats Domino was playing at the Flamingo. Back when I started at Decca, a Fats Domino EP had been one of the first records I put together. John, too, was a huge fan.

When we got to the Flamingo, we were ushered backstage to meet Fats, and we both felt a little starstruck. His hands, I remember, were festooned with diamond rings that glistened in the light. John was in a playful mood and knelt down before him, kissing his hands.

'I should be kissing your hand,' Fats said.

'No way,' said John. 'You are the king, the person I have come to pay homage to.'

Fats was amazing. The show was good, the atmosphere was great, and the drinks were flowing. So much so that by the time Fats departed, to be followed by Frankie Valli, John was getting louder and louder, and drunker and drunker. The security guards were beginning to take notice of us, and I thought, *This is going to kick off at some point.* Sure enough, John started heckling.

'Get your cock out, Frankie!' he shouted.

At which point the security guards started to come over. John looked at me and said, in this funny little voice, 'Time to go?'

'Definitely,' I said.

I grabbed him, and we ran out into the lobby and then into the night. We crossed over the road, back towards Caesar's Palace, and for a moment I thought I'd lost him. Then I realised he'd stopped to take a piss against one of the trees that were planted in front of the hotel. I got him into the lobby, whereupon he started grabbing casino chips and throwing them all over the place. *Time for bed*, I thought. Together with May, I bundled him into an elevator and got him back to their room. I pushed John onto the bed, rolled him over so he was on his back and pulled his cowboy boots off. Then I turned to May and said, 'He's all yours.'

The following day, it was time to head back to LA. John decided that rather than catching a flight, he'd like to drive back, so he and May joined me in the Thunderbird, and we headed out across the desert, *Thelma and Louise* style. As we were driving, we came across Calico, a former mining community that had been abandoned in the 1890s, ending up as a sort of ghost town. I pulled over, and we had a look around. We found a stall selling Native American headdresses, which we bought, and May took photos of the pair of us. I still have them: they're lovely, capturing two friends having a good time.

Many years later, when I was working with Elton on his Las Vegas show, Brandon Flowers, the lead singer of the Killers, came to see the performance, and I got chatting to him backstage. Brandon lives in Vegas and asked if I'd been there before. So I explained how, several decades before, I'd gone there with John.

'Did you know that there's a famous story of John Lennon visiting Calico, the desert town?' Brandon asked.

'Yes,' I said. 'I took him there.'

Brandon double-blinked at that, and did so again as I got my phone out and showed him the photos.

'You do realise that's a legendary story around these parts?' Brandon said.

I could see he was hugely impressed. And every time I've seen him since, he always brings up the story.

———

The look I saw between John and Yoko backstage at Elton John's Madison Square Garden concert wasn't the moment when they got back together, but it was a flash, a sign that there was still something between them. When they eventually reunited, it wasn't a huge surprise to me, and my relationship with John became one with both of them.

John moved back to New York in mid-1974. Phil Spector had been injured in a car accident, and the *Rock 'n' Roll* sessions had been paused. Back in New York, John began work instead on what would become the *Walls and Bridges* album, from which 'Whatever Gets You Thru the Night' was taken. *Rock 'n' Roll* was released the following year, after a bit more recording and tidying up. Even that was complicated: there was an ongoing legal dispute with Morris Levy, a publisher, who attempted to put out his own version of the album, called *Roots: John Lennon Sings the Great Rock & Roll Hits*.

Even though John was back in New York, and back together with Yoko, his wild, rebellious streak was not entirely dimmed. In 1975, he was invited to present the Record of the Year award with Paul Simon at that year's Grammys. John asked me what I thought he should do.

'It's the smartest thing you could do,' I told him. With the FBI's interest still lingering in the background, it would give him cover. 'It's an appearance on national television. No one is going to throw you out of the country when you've just done that.'

John was on great form that night. He was in a playful mood, and he and Paul Simon joked around on stage about former band members and reunions. When Art Garfunkel was called up on stage to accept an award on behalf of the absent Olivia Newton-John, Simon quipped, 'I thought I told you to wait in the car.'

Afterwards, there was a star-studded party. I was at a table with John and Yoko, when John disappeared. Yoko and I carried on talking, but after a while, Yoko began to look concerned.

'Tony, can you go and find John for me?' she asked.

I went off in search of John, eventually finding him in the gentlemen's toilets with David Bowie. John and David got on well: John loved David's *Young Americans* album, and had ended up co-writing and singing on one of the album's biggest hits, 'Fame'. (I was a huge Bowie fan, too. Back in 1973, I had been lucky enough to go to the famous Ziggy Stardust concert at the Hammersmith Odeon, and it remains one of the most amazing shows I have ever seen.)

As talented as David was, he was also someone whom Yoko regarded it as necessary to keep an eye on. By 1975, David was doing a lot of cocaine, and when I found him and John together in the toilets, sure enough, that's what the two of them were up to.

'Red alert, John,' I said.

John looked up at me. 'Is it Mother?' he asked, using his name for Yoko.

I nodded. 'Yes, she is looking for you.'

John looked over at David. 'I had better go back then,' he shrugged, and he went to rejoin Yoko, who was perhaps none the wiser.

———

I wouldn't want you to get the wrong impression about Yoko, though. When John got back together with her, I began to really get to know her properly. She is a unique individual and has a great sense of humour. I always used to say to John, 'She is so funny.' And John would reply, 'I know. People don't get her.'

There was an occasion when a meeting was arranged with Bob Mercer, a record company guy who was over from the UK. John, Yoko and I had planned to take some mushrooms that day, before the meeting had been put in place. I explained the situation to Yoko, who thought about it for a second, then said, 'Well, we can still take them anyway.'

The three of us took the mushrooms before the meeting. Poor Bob. We were flying and couldn't stop laughing. I remember Yoko turning to me and saying across the table, 'Good, aren't they?' I was thinking, *Oh my* God! I was so high, I've no idea how I managed to eat my meal.

I remember hitting Bob up for a trip back to London so I could do some work on John's behalf. 'It would be very good if the record company were to ask me over to London to sort things out,' I said, to giggles from the others. I was so high, I thought I had better do something that came across as sensible and business-minded. Bob agreed, and we all laughed some more.

Yoko was funny in all sorts of ways. The first time I went to their apartment at the Dakota building, she showed me around her dressing room. She had rows of sweaters, the same ones in three different sizes.

'I can never decide which size is going to fit me,' she explained, 'so I always order three.'

John and Yoko owned a herd of Friesian cattle in upstate New York. Years later, after John's death, I remember meeting up with Yoko and asking if she still kept their country place. 'Oh yes,' she said, 'I go up there at weekends. I love it.'

'And do you still have the cattle?'

'Oh no.' Yoko shook her head. 'All that mooing.'

She was very particular about the apartment. One time, I saw a glass of water and, trying to be helpful, washed it up. Yoko came back and asked where the glass was. When I told her what I'd done, she said, 'No, that was a piece of artwork.' I remember John roaring with laughter because Yoko's art had been washed up.

Yoko had an eye for art even in the everyday. When she became pregnant with Sean, she was told by doctors to spend time resting in bed and not to walk about; the only way she could get from the bed to the kitchen was by wheelchair. One day, she rang to say that she was having a refrigerator delivered, and could I help them install it? 'Sure,' I said. The delivery men arrived, and the refrigerator was huge – like the ones you get in the supermarket with the sliding doors. Getting the fridge to the kitchen was no easy task: the glass of water I'd washed up by mistake was not the only work of art by Yoko in the house. In the corridor sat an armchair that she had wrapped in bandages. I looked at the delivery men and said, 'Whatever you do, don't touch that.'

I got the fridge installed all fine and went to tell Yoko.

'Let me see,' she said.

I helped her into the wheelchair and wheeled her into the kitchen. Yoko took a look and said to me, 'OK, now we arrange the food.'

'OK . . .' I said, bemused.

And for the next hour or so, Yoko sat there in the wheelchair, art-directing. 'I want the tomatoes here . . . No, try them on that shelf . . . Put the milk there . . . Let's see where we can put the carrots.' By the end, I have to admit it did look rather beautiful.

John came back – I can't remember where he'd been – and immediately went to get something to eat.

'Don't go near the fridge,' Yoko said sharply.

Top: With Mum, Aunty Gladys and Dad at the seaside

Bottom: St Andrew's Junior School picture, aged eight or nine

Top: With my brother Peter and biological mother, Kay,
Eastbourne seafront

Bottom: In the back garden in Eastbourne, with Chico the family dog

Top: With Peter and Kay, Eastbourne seafront

Bottom: With Mum and Dad in the back garden, 1961

Aged fifteen

Top: In L'Estartit, Spain, 1966

Bottom: With my biological father, Hughie, late 1980s

Top: With Neil Sedaka

Bottom: With Brenda Lee, mid-1960s

Top: With the Ronettes, Phil Spector, George Harrison
and Tony Hall *(far right)*, 1964

Bottom: With Roy Orbison, mid-1960s

Top: With Ketty Lester, my first plugging success

Bottom: With Pattie Harrison, on the way to the
'All You Need Is Love' recording, June 1967

John looked at me. 'We've been art-directing,' I explained.

He laughed and left the fridge alone.

———

Yoko's pregnancy with Sean marked a change in John's life. As I said earlier, he'd really liked David Bowie's *Young Americans* album and wanted to explore the possibility of creating something similar. We were talking about hiring a group of Black musicians in New York to make what for John would be a different sort of record. We even had a title for it: 'Between the Lines'. But then Yoko became pregnant. I met up with John for coffee at Rumpelmayer's in the centre of Park South, and he told me he'd decided not to make the album after all. He explained how Yoko had been told to rest and stay in bed if she was to have any chance of keeping the baby.

'I am going to stay at home and be a house husband,' he said.

The last time I saw John was in 1976, on my birthday. I went to the Dakota to have breakfast with them. John and Yoko were on a no-sugar kick at the time, and they gave me a copy of *Sugar Blues* by William Duffy, which was all about the evils of sugar. We had breakfast, sugar-free, and then went out for a walk. We ended up in an antiques shop, and Yoko wandered around, pointing at different items: 'I like that, and I like that . . .' As we left, I went up to the shop assistant to explain her behaviour. 'Don't worry,' he said, 'we know them.' By the time we got back to the apartment, everything that Yoko had pointed at was there waiting for her so she could pick out what she wanted to buy.

John was true to his word about becoming a house husband. He never did things by halves, and he devoted himself to Yoko and his son, to the point where he cut himself off from everyone else in order to do so. Being suddenly dropped like that hurt.

I'd come to New York and had basically been told that John was raising Sean and didn't want to see his friends. I wrote him a note, telling him how upset I was. He didn't take kindly to that, but it was true: we had done so much together, and suddenly he didn't want to know.

On the day before John was tragically shot, he did an interview with the BBC. He was asked how he knew Elton John. 'We have a mutual friend, Tony King,' John explained. I can't explain how much those words have meant to me since then. The fact that he described me as a friend, the day before his death, means everything.

One of my favourite John songs is 'Bless You', off *Walls and Bridges*. I love the lyrics and I love what I have always thought is an obvious dedication to Yoko. There is such tenderness in his voice. Listen to the song, and you can hear that he is singing it and really meaning it. That is the John Lennon I remember through and through: a beautiful, tender, special man.

9

I had been fortunate to be Elton John's friend before he actually became Elton. It meant we knew the friendship was true, rather than one based on his subsequent success. We connected from the off, and that was the bedrock. And when he became successful, he was always incredibly generous and wanted to share that success with me. The result has been one of the most important relationships of my life, one where we still speak most days. I feel incredibly privileged to know him.

Over the years, we have done so many fun things together that it is difficult to know where to begin. But perhaps we should start on a train from London to Leeds, on our way to see Dusty Springfield perform at Batley Variety Club. It might seem strange looking back now, but at the time the club was dubbed the 'Las Vegas of the North', with the original designers apparently having travelled to Nevada for inspiration. Between 1967 and 1978, the venue played host to a number of major acts, including Louis Armstrong, Tom Jones, Shirley Bassey and my old friend Roy Orbison, who recorded a live album there in 1969.

We were taking the train up north with another friend, Mike Gill, who was also gay, and who worked as a publicist for Rod Stewart. We piled our luggage in – we were going for only one night but seemed to have ended up with suitcase after suitcase. Once the train pulled out, we started to drink. We bought and drank every single miniature that was available. All of a sudden – or at least it felt like that – the train stopped. As we were

125

chatting, I saw a sign on the platform that said 'LEEDS'.

'Oh my God,' I said, pointing out the sign to the others. 'We're here.'

We opened the windows (this was one of those old British Rail trains) and started throwing our suitcases onto the platform. Then the three of us piled out, three desperate gay guys falling out of the train. Elton, if I remember rightly, was wearing a red fox-fur coat. We didn't look very Leeds, put it that way.

Elton had ordered a limousine to take us from the station to our hotel, and thankfully it was there waiting for us. We threw our suitcases into the back and clambered in.

'The Queens Hotel,' Elton said, with a flourish.

The limousine driver doffed his cap and set off. Fifty yards later, he pulled up.

'What are you doing?' I asked. 'Why have you stopped?'

'We're here, sir,' the driver said, pointing out of the window.

Sure enough, there was a big sign saying 'Queens Hotel'. We clambered out again, grabbed our suitcases and checked in.

Being friends with Elton during this period was madcap, unpredictable and the greatest fun. If we weren't going to Batley, we were going for drinks with royalty. In 1974, he played a gig at the Festival Hall, and afterwards we were invited to Princess Margaret's for drinks. A whole group of us went along for the ride. I always remember that Linda Stein, the wife of music mogul Seymour Stein, couldn't believe that Princess Margaret had plastic matting below the bar. The Queen famously had her Tupperware, but I can report that her sister had her own share of plastic.

At the time the princess was going through a difficult patch in her marriage to Tony Armstrong-Jones. He turned up late with a group of young friends and was quite surly and offhand. 'Don't be so tiresome,' I remember her telling him.

Margaret had her eye on me, meanwhile, but for different reasons. I was wearing a white suit, and if I say so myself, was looking rather dashing. I got talking to some youngblood – I can't remember his title, but he was an earl or something like that. We were getting on well and having a really interesting conversation, when the princess called him over and dismissed him. She sent him home. I think she thought I was trying to pick him up, which I wasn't. But, clearly, she wasn't taking any chances!

On another occasion, Elton and I went to meet Mae West in her LA apartment at the Ravenswood (West famously bought the building when the owners stopped her then boyfriend, the African American boxer William Jones, from entering). A whole group of us were invited, and when she appeared in the doorway, she looked us up and down and said, 'My favourite sight – wall to wall men.'

There was a time, too, when Elton and I went to see Frank Sinatra. We got invited backstage, and I had a really nice chat with him. Frank was a seriously good-looking guy, with a real twinkle in his eye. Later, when he did the gig, he sang 'Sorry Seems to Be the Hardest Word'. Elton and I were in the front row, and he sang the song looking straight at us. Elton nudged me and asked, 'Do you think he is singing this to us?'

'It very much looks like it,' I replied.

Elton is a hugely social person. When he was in a relationship with his manager, John Reid, they would go out a lot, and there'd be dinners with a whole range of people. I introduced him to Charlie and Shirley Watts, and we'd go out with them. On another occasion, we went out to dinner with David and Angie Bowie. Elton would buy me gifts, and he went through a period when he would deliberately choose things that were in the worst taste, such as a garish sign that said 'Singapore' in illuminated letters on a black velvet background. I wore an earring at the time, so he also bought me an ornament of a parrot on a perch. In the end, I had to say, 'Will you stop doing this? I'm so loaded up with them, I don't know what to do with them.' I had to start giving them away.

But he gave me amazing presents, too. When I was working at Apple, he'd come to see me, in the same way that he used call in when I was working for George Martin at AIR. He became a bit of fixture at Apple – everyone on the switchboard knew him. He'd say hello to everyone, and then we'd go out and have lunch at Prunier's, a fantastic restaurant in St James's that he liked. That was where Elton told me he'd received his first royalty cheque, and that suddenly he was worth a lot of money. He was thrilled and said, 'Let's go and spend some of it.' We finished lunch and went to Cartier, where he bought me the most beautiful ring, which I have kept ever since.

Despite the money and success, Elton still remained unsure of his own ability sometimes. One day, he came into the Apple office, having just finished recording. 'I've got my new single with me,' he said, 'but I'm not sure about it. Can I play it to you?'

Elton often played me new stuff, so we sat down together to listen.

'What's the song called?' I asked.

'"Don't Let the Sun Go Down on Me",' Elton said.

We listened in silence. I was blown away. When the song finished, I looked at him and said, 'You're not sure?'

Elton shook his head. 'No, I'm not really. When I first heard it back, I chucked it across the room and said, "Give it to Engelbert Humperdinck."'

'You're kidding me,' I said. 'That's a monster hit if ever I heard one.'

Elton still didn't look convinced, so I took him up to see Ringo. Elton and Ringo had a lot of respect and time for each other.

A couple of years later, we'd take a crazy, drug-fuelled trip to Amsterdam together. Elton was out there rehearsing, and Ringo and I were doing some promotional work, so we met up with him and John Reid and enjoyed a bizarre, stoned canal-boat ride. Everyone was doing blowback, where you blow the spliff smoke into someone else's mouth. When we got back to the hotel, we sat in the lobby, completely out of it. There was a pianist playing who wasn't very good, so to stop him John decided to pay him off. The ploy worked.

Back at Apple, Elton and I sat in Ringo's office and listened to 'Don't Let the Sun Go Down on Me' again. When it finished, Ringo looked at Elton and said, 'That is a monster hit. You can't doubt yourself on this one.'

'I told you,' I said to Elton.

Ringo and I were proved right, and after that, Elton would often dedicate the song to me.

————

In 1973, Elton flew me to California for a holiday. We stayed in Beverly Hills, in this amazing property that used to belong to Joan Collins and Anthony Newley, before they split up; later on, it would be owned by Fleetwood Mac's Christine McVie.

It was during this trip that I took Elton to his first gay bar. Up to that point, it wasn't something he'd ever been interested in. I'd found out about the bar from Elton's hairdresser, who was there to make Elton's hair and eyebrows pink. As this guy was doing the colouring, I sat with Elton, keeping him company and chatting away – we could talk for hours. I didn't really know California at this point, so I asked the hairdresser if he could recommend any places where we could go out and dance.

'There's a great place called After Dark on Melrose and Beverly,' the hairdresser suggested.

Elton said to me, 'Maybe you can go there one night.' Then he added, 'Of course, I won't be coming.'

I felt a bit bad for asking, seeing as I was on holiday with him. 'I would like to have a look at it, if that's OK,' I said.

'No, that's fine,' Elton reassured me.

That night, we all went out for dinner. I drove there separately, in this beautiful blue Cadillac that Elton had hired for me, so I could go on to the bar afterwards. We had a really jolly meal, and at the end of it, Elton asked, 'Are you going to your club now?'

'You bet,' I nodded. 'I'm really in the mood for it.'

Then, to my surprise, Elton said, 'Do you think I should come with you?'

I looked at him, as I knew that would be a big deal for him. 'That is up to you, Elton,' I said.

Elton thought for a moment. 'Well, I am curious,' he said.

'I'll tell you what,' I said. 'Why don't you go in for five minutes and take the vibe? If it doesn't feel good to you, you can just leave. You've popped in and out again – no big deal. It doesn't make you part of the gay fraternity if you spend five minutes in a gay bar.'

Elton felt reassured by that, so he, John Reid and I went to the club. As we walked in, the DJ was spinning 'I'll Always Love My Mama' by the Intruders, an amazing early disco song that was streets ahead of its time. 'What *is* that song?' Elton mouthed at me. Next up was 'Honey Bee' by Gloria Gaynor, another huge early disco tune.

'Well?' I asked, as we walked over to the bar.

'Well, I can't leave now,' Elton said. 'The music is too good.'

As we stood there drinking, a number of guys came over to introduce themselves, all very polite: 'Hi, Elton, it's nice to see you here' – that sort of thing. It was all very friendly and relaxed. Elton turned to me and said, 'It's nice here, isn't it? It's got a good atmosphere.'

'A great atmosphere,' I replied, noticing that the bartender had clocked me. I went on to pick him up: he came back to the house and took me to a nudist beach the following day.

The following night, Elton, John and I were back in After Dark, and we would go there almost every night of the holiday. When I moved to California, it became a bit of a regular haunt. We took all sorts of people. Mike Maitland, the straight-as-a-die head of MCA Records, had a great time. Billie Jean King came on another occasion. And, most memorably, we once took Dusty Springfield – the venue was slightly different to Batley Variety Club! When we invited her, she said, 'Usually I need two days' notice before I go out.'

When we got to After Dark, Dusty declared, 'I need some hairspray,' and asked me to go with her to a pharmacist's on the opposite side of the road. I walked in with her, all the way to the back, where the hairspray was. She picked up a can, gave it a shake and then walked back to the front desk, holding her finger down on the button the whole way, with me following behind in this huge mist. When we got outside, she gave me a brush and said, 'Can you sort my hair out at the back?' I tried, but with the amount of spray she'd just put on it, it was like concrete! So I tapped it a couple of times, said it was fine, and we headed in. Inside, Dusty had a great time. In fact, she had such a great time that when we took her back to the Sunset Marquis in West Hollywood, she was so drunk she fell out of the taxi, and I had to help her inside.

The trips to After Dark weren't the only reason the holiday was so memorable. It was during this break that I introduced Elton to the tennis legend Billie Jean King. I've always been a huge fan of the sport, ever since I was a young lad. I used to be a ball boy for the Davis Cup matches when they were played in Eastbourne, and also for the South of England Tennis Championships (I got a pound a week and free sandwiches). I'd be crouched at the net, scampering back and forth when a serve didn't go over. When the games finished, I'd run back home to watch myself on TV.

Elton and I were at a Hollywood party, when we spotted Billie Jean across the room. In 1973, she was at the peak of her success and was known as Queen Billie Jean. She won the singles, women's doubles and mixed doubles at Wimbledon that year, and famously defeated Bobby Riggs in the so-called Battle of the Sexes match. She was on one side of the room, and Elton and I were on the other. I could see both of them looking at each other like two shy teenagers. Eventually, I went over to talk to Billie Jean myself. I pointed over and said, 'You know, I'm sure Elton would love to meet you.' Billie Jean's response was, 'I am too shy.' So I grabbed her by the hand and took her over. From that moment on, they were firm friends.

My role in their relationship wasn't quite over, however. The following year, it was arranged that Elton and Billie Jean would do a photoshoot with photographer Terry O'Neill, when Billie Jean was over for Wimbledon. When the day came, however, Elton had taken some Mandrax the night before and completely overslept, and didn't want to go. Terry rang me up and asked if there was anything I could do to persuade him to come. (I often got asked to do the persuading!) I went to see Elton and told him we couldn't let Billie Jean down, and that he had to go. He grumbled a bit at first but eventually agreed, and the photo session turned out to be great and the pictures fabulous.

One night during the holiday, we had a conversation about Elton playing the Hollywood Bowl. I can't remember who, but someone had the idea of all these different people coming on dressed as the Queen, the Pope and various other characters. I assumed it was one of those holiday conversations and thought no more about it. But when I got back to the UK, the idea began to take shape and a date was set.

On the day of the show, I'd flown back to Los Angeles to work on Ringo's latest album. I'd just got to Mike Hazlewood's house, when I got a call from John Reid.

'You're there,' he said. 'Thank goodness. I'm sending a limo round for you.'

'Why?' I asked.

'I want you to go on stage at the Hollywood Bowl tonight,' John said. 'I've arranged for Linda Lovelace to introduce Elton, and I want you to introduce Linda. Elton doesn't know you're here, so I want it all to be a big surprise.'

The whole evening was totally surreal. The limo pulled up, and inside was movie director John Schlesinger and his boyfriend. I was dressed in a sharp blue Tommy Nutter suit and a sequinned tie that Ringo's wife, Maureen, had made for me. *This is crazy*, I thought, as the limo drove to the venue. *I've just got off a flight from London, and now I'm going to walk out at an Elton John concert and introduce Linda Lovelace.*

Linda had become a worldwide celebrity and was the most famous pornographic actress of the time, thanks to her starring role in the 1972 film *Deep Throat. How on earth do I introduce her?* I wondered. In the end, I described her as 'that well-known naughty girl'. I didn't really know what else to say. On came this strange cast list of characters we'd brainstormed, and then Linda herself introduced Elton, who descended the stairs at the back of the stage wearing a remarkable silver-trousered, white-feathered outfit. Then the cast of characters opened five different coloured pianos, each one with a letter from Elton's name on the lid, out of which were meant to fly a spectacular gaggle of doves. Some did, though many of them stayed put! Even so, as far as stage entrances went, it didn't get much more dramatic or glamorous than this.

———

During the Hollywood holiday, Elton had an acetate of *Goodbye Yellow Brick Road*, which he'd play for anyone who came round. As soon as I heard it, I was blown away. I'd loved all his albums up to that point – *Madman Across the Water, Honky Château, Don't Shoot Me, I'm Only the Piano Player* and the others – but this was something else. When I heard it, I thought, *Oh hello. This is his* Sergeant Pepper, *his* Exile on Main Street, *his signature album.*

It's difficult to imagine now just how big *Goodbye Yellow Brick Road* was when it was first released. It was everywhere in America that year. Radio played the hell out of the album. Everywhere you went, every time you got in a taxi, another track from the record was being played.

The tour to support the album was in some ways probably the pinnacle of his career. Elton used to get carried on stage on the shoulders of Mr Universe. The noise when he appeared was deafening. I remember going to watch him in Los Angeles with Ringo Starr. When Elton started playing the opening of 'Funeral for a Friend', the volume from the crowd was ear-splitting. It was fitting I was with Ringo: I hadn't heard a noise like that since those early Beatles concerts.

I saw Elton at his Dodger Stadium shows in 1975, when he was the first act to play there since, yes, the Beatles. The week before, his star had been unveiled on the Hollywood Walk of Fame, and he'd flown a load of family and friends over on a chartered plane;

we met them at the airport with a fleet of limousines. His new album, *Rock of the Westies*, had gone straight in at number one – not even the Beatles had managed that. Maybe this was all too much and too overwhelming for him, because what happened next was shocking: he took an overdose of Valium, attempting to commit suicide. It perhaps wasn't a serious attempt, by which I mean he only had to be given something to make him throw up in order to survive, but even if he hadn't tried to kill himself, it was definitely a cry for help.

I was called up to go over and see him. I went straight to the house. I had a whole mixture of emotions churning inside me, but when I saw him sat up in bed, my heart melted a little.

'Are you ready for what I've got to say?' I asked.

Elton just said, 'Not really.'

'All right,' I said. 'Then I won't be too hard.' I looked at him and shook my head. 'What are you up to, Elton? What are you doing this for? You've got two huge shows in a couple of days.'

'I know,' Elton said. But we chatted, and I hope I helped to pull him back from wherever he had got himself to. Elton sorted himself out: as much as he could go down, his ability to bounce back up was always extraordinary. The shows were back on.

I went to watch the rehearsals. I was with Robert Hilburn, the American music critic who had reviewed Elton's breakthrough shows at the Troubadour back in 1970. We climbed up and watched the rehearsals from the back, all the way up in the stands at the opposite side of the stadium. Even with no fans, the sound was amazing, echoing around; when the stadium was full, the atmosphere was electric. With Cary Grant backstage and Billie Jean King on backing vocals, the shows were something special. You'd never have known what Elton had been through over the previous few days.

When John Lennon stopped recording and devoted himself to Yoko and Sean, I needed a new job. That came with Rocket Records, Elton's label, where I was made executive vice president.

Elton was by far the biggest act on the label. In one way, it was strange to formalise our friendship into a working one, but in another, it was a natural extension of how we had bounced ideas off each other for years. At the end of 1975, Elton invited me to come and spend Christmas with him in Barbados. There was a whole gang of us: Elton and John Reid, myself, David Nutter, Bernie Taupin, Kiki Dee, Oliver Messel and others. We had a wonderful time, with lots of fun dinners. And Elton was on great form. He had come off the booze and was glowing with health.

He went straight from Barbados to the studio, where he recorded his next album, *Blue Moves*. He was sober throughout the sessions, which is why his voice is so beautiful on that record. Listen to 'Idol', my favourite song on the album, and you can hear the purity and trademark tone of his singing.

I worked hard on that record with him. We arranged for David Nutter to take photos. I sorted out the artwork and brought Tom Moulton in to do a dance remix of 'Bite Your Lip (Get Up and Dance)'. I sorted out the promotion: the usual circus of interviews and arranging for critics to listen to the album. They liked the record, and the reviews were good, but even though *Blue Moves* got to number one in the US, it didn't set the world on fire like the previous albums. There was only one real bona fide smash on the record: 'Sorry Seems to Be the Hardest Word'.

Towards the end of the accompanying tour, Elton did an interview with Cliff Jahr, a journalist from *Rolling Stone*. In the interview they talked about Elton's sexuality, and he said he was bisexual.

He hadn't really spoken about his sexuality publicly before, and I remember John Reid being furious with him for having done so. Lots of people at Rocket were really worried about what it might do to his career, such was the climate of homophobia at the time, and he got dropped by a number of radio stations in the States. In the UK, the *Sun* cancelled a competition to win copies of *Blue Moves*, on the spurious basis that the album cover featured only men and no women. But for all the concerns, Elton was relieved to have said it, and he did say 'bisexual' rather than 'gay', which was the safest step forward at the time, and probably as much as he could say, being the big star he was at the time.

Rocket had a great roster of artists to work with, as well as Elton – Neil Sedaka, Lulu, Kiki Dee . . . One of the biggest successes I had was breaking Cliff Richard in the States. Although Cliff had been a huge star around the world for years, he'd never been able to crack America. But 'Devil Woman' was a brilliant record, and I was able to help him get the recognition he deserved.

I took Cliff on a three-week tour around the States to promote the record. Breaking a song in America isn't an easy thing to do: you have to put in the time and the miles to build up the goodwill. Rather than it being a single market like in the UK, the States is made up of lots of different regional markets, and you have to work the radio stations and do press in each one. You can only do that on the ground, by getting out there and going to Portland, Seattle, Chicago, Memphis, Nashville, Atlanta and so on. By doing so you build up goodwill, and if you've got a good record behind you, as Cliff had, then those local radio stations will add you to their playlists. That was the goal of the campaign: to build up those playlist 'adds'.

One of the biggest radio networks was RKO, run by a brilliant guy called Paul Drew. I got on well with him and his wife, Ann, and they used to invite me round for dinner. When they were stuck for a cleaning lady, I recommended my own. All of which might not sound like much, but such was Paul's clout that half the record industry was beating down his door to get a meeting with him, and there I was, having dinner at his house. (One of my biggest regrets was a dinner Paul invited me to along with Barbra Streisand, and having to say no because I had a work event and couldn't make it.)

Paul knew I was working the Cliff Richard record hard, but he and I both knew that he wouldn't give me a break until he could see that the record had legs. That was where the tour of the different markets came in and accumulating the 'adds'. He waited and waited, and then, when he saw it was breaking in enough markets, he added it to the playlist on WABC, the RKO station in Boston. Once the record was on one RKO station's playlist, the rest followed like dominoes. That was how you got a hit record in the US, where, unlike in the UK, the charts at the time were based on both sales and radio airplay. You couldn't have a hit without the radio playing your song. I remember that when I worked on John Lennon's 'Mind Games', Paul didn't think the song was commercial enough. It was never added to the RKO playlists and stalled at number eighteen as a result.

Cliff's manager was a guy called Peter Gormley, whom I'd known for years. He worked up the road from me when I was working for Apple in Savile Row. As well as Cliff, he also managed Olivia Newton-John. When I was working on George Harrison's album *All Things Must Pass*, Peter rang me up and asked if there was anything good on it that might be suitable for Olivia to sing. I thought about it and suggested 'If Not for You', George's cover of the Bob Dylan song. I took it down the road so Peter could listen to it. He loved it, got Olivia to record it, and it became her

With Elton, 1973

Dressing up in a photo booth with John Lennon,
Lexington Avenue, 1975

With John in Calico, on our way back from Las Vegas, 1973

Top: Backstage at Madison Square Garden with John
and Ray Cooper, 1974

Bottom: With John and Elton, on our way to Boston, 1974

Top: Rehearsals for the Madison Square Garden show, 1974

Bottom: The *Mind Games* advert shoot, with John, 1973

With Freddie, 1981

With Mick Jagger, 1987

Top: Backstage with Keith Richards and Ronnie Wood

Bottom: With Charlie Watts, 1995

first hit. (In a similar way, I also had a hand in Kiki Dee's first hit, 'Amoureuse'. I loved the French version by Véronique Sanson and played it to Elton. He then asked Gary Osborne to write some English lyrics and got Kiki to record it.)

Peter found the idea of Cliff touring America with an openly gay man really amusing. He wasn't sure how that might work, but Cliff and I got along like a house on fire. He thought I was hilarious and incredibly easy company. We gossiped away on flights and talked about all sorts of topics: God, sex, everything.

Every day on the tour, we'd host a reception where we'd meet DJs and music people. Cliff was great at doing the 'meet and greet' and looked forward to it. We'd get towards five o'clock, and he'd ask, 'Is it time for the wine yet?'

'Yes, Cliff,' I'd reply. 'I think it is wine time.'

We ended up back in LA after the three weeks, and Peter said to me, 'Cliff is so different, having had a dose of you for three weeks. You have affected him in a very positive way.'

I was happy to help Cliff. He's someone who has been a bit overlooked musically, although he's done some great songs over the years. 'Move It' was one of my jukebox favourites when I was sixteen. 'Miss You Nights' is a beautiful song. 'We Don't Talk Anymore' is a great number as well. Years later, I had dinner with him, at the time when he was dealing with all those horrible accusations from the BBC. John Reid held a dinner party for him, and he invited me along. When I saw him, I could see how bruised he'd been by the experience. He was a changed man – I could see it in his face. But I hope that having another dose of me was some small comfort in such difficult times.

10

Once I'd been to California for the first time, I always dreamed of going back. Joni Mitchell's song from the time, 'Court and Spark', worked as a beckoning finger, compelling me to return. 'I couldn't let go of LA,' as Joni sang.

Everything seemed bigger and brighter and sunnier and more colourful in California. It might seem like a small detail, but one of the things I remember about LA was having a walk-in shower. Back in London, I'd been sharing a flat just off Baker Street, where I used to have to sit in the bath and hold the shower attachment over my head. To move to California and have my own walk-in shower made it feel as though I'd made it! I got myself a Mercedes – Los Angeles is all about cars – and that reinforced the sentiment.

One of my early Californian friends was Dennis Killeen. Dennis worked for Capitol, and I knew him from having worked on Ringo Starr's albums: I had a corner of his desk and would work from that. Once I moved to LA properly, we became fast friends – and still are. I remember going to watch *Jaws* with him when it first came out. Dennis said he was going with a couple of friends of his, Michael Harris and his boyfriend Lee, and asked if I'd like to come along. When I got to the cinema, Michael and Lee showed up in leather. *OK*, I said to myself. *Tough guys, leather*. We went in to watch the film, and every time there was a frightening part, I grabbed Michael's arm, which he found hilarious.

I became good friends with Michael after that. He was a proper local and knew all the important details about the city that only those in the know are aware of: the burrito stand downtown that made the greatest burritos you've ever tasted in your life; the time when one should drive out into the desert to see the desert flowers at their best. Michael was a very stylish guy. I visited his apartment once, and that was the first time I'd properly come across minimalism. He had all his photos on the floor, lined up against the wall, and I thought, *Why doesn't he just hang them?* And then I realised that was part of the look.

He was a man of extreme moods. Sometimes he would ring me up and say, 'I am really depressed today.' To which I'd answer, 'Fancy coming out for a Mexican and giving your depression a two-hour break?' And we'd meet up at a nearby restaurant called Lucy's, where we'd have a couple of margaritas, a great dinner and a laugh. Then he'd go back home and snuggle up under his comforter with his bad mood. One of the many things I loved about Michael was that he had a very measured view on things. He was never outright critical, but would always say, 'Well, Tony, maybe you should think about this . . .' and offer up an alternative point of view. I could be quite opinionated in those days, but Michael slowed me down and made me think.

One day I'll always remember is when we went down to Laguna Beach to see a friend of his, Russell. It was a misty day, and I remember him playing *The Köln Concert* by Keith Jarrett – an amazing piano performance that became one of my favourite records. Whenever I hear it now, I always think back to Laguna. It's a beautiful little beach community, with lovely houses. A friend of mine, Bruce, built an amazing home there. He built it around a tree, so that the tree grew in a well in the centre of the house. He put a frosted-glass ceiling on the bathroom, so when the sun came out, the shadows of the tree's leaves were reflected down. It was really clever, and that sort of design and creativity summed up Laguna.

It was a very artistic place. They had a gay bar called the Little Shrimp, where someone sat at the piano singing songs. I remember going to a fantastic Halloween drag party there: they had a huge crate of women's clothes, and you had to pick something out and put it on.

To begin with, I really loved the Californian lifestyle. I liked its pace and its laid-back nature. I tried to get the LA look. There was a nonchalance to how people dressed so casually, and I tried to copy that: khaki trousers and a casual shirt, or a pair of jeans and a T-shirt. But I did get a bit fed up about not being able to walk anywhere. The only time you'd bump into people was at a stop light or in a supermarket. One of the older guys who worked at Capitol told me how he'd bumped into Marilyn Monroe that way. He'd gone into a 7/11, and there was Marilyn, dressed in a mink coat and black wig, doing a bit of late-night shopping. He went up to her and said, 'Oh, hi, Marilyn, how are you?' And Marilyn replied, in that whispery voice of hers, 'How did you know it was me?'

I saw so many amazing concerts while I was there. I was at Santa Barbara to see Fleetwood Mac in their heyday; I also saw Linda Ronstadt and Joni Mitchell, both at the Universal Amphitheatre, in the open air; Bruce Springsteen at the Roxy; Boz Scaggs, Bonnie Raitt, Bob Seger, the Stones, the Eagles . . . everyone.

And the people I got to meet . . . One time, I received an invitation to go to dinner with Liberace, who was charm personified. When I got there, I realised that a number of other glamorous young men had been invited. They were great-looking but, being young, had less to say than me. Because of my career, I had more to talk about, and Liberace and I ended up having a really good conversation. I asked him if he had any hobbies. 'Yes,' he told me. 'I buy homes, then fill them with antiques.' I asked what happened when the home was full. He shrugged: 'I buy another one.'

I also got to know Peter Asher, who produced Linda Ronstadt and managed Joni Mitchell. He and his wife, Betsy, would have these amazing gatherings. Their house was like a salon. It was where I met Jack Nicholson, Michelle from the Mamas and the Papas, Linda Ronstadt, Carly Simon, James Taylor, Don Henley.

When I saw Linda Ronstadt at the Universal Amphitheatre, she decided to come on stage dressed in a Girl Scouts outfit. She was also wearing a gardenia that I'd sent her, and halfway through the set she said to the crowd, 'Do you like my gardenia? My friend Tony King sent it to me.' As you can imagine, I was made up by that.

Backstage afterwards, I was still basking in the moment. I was with Betsy, Peter and a few others, and I said, 'Did you hear my dedication? She dedicated that song to me after mentioning the flower.'

Betsy turned round and said, 'How thoughtful of you to remind us all.' Which was a very Betsy thing to say!

I also met Joni Mitchell quite a few times with Betsy, and I was always so excited. She is my idol, really. Her music truly touches my heart. She has this extraordinary way of pulling out these fantastic lines and lyrics that are so profound. Seeing her at the Universal Amphitheatre was a bit like seeing Elton on his Goodbye Yellow Brick Road tour – a great artist at the peak of their powers. Joni played 'A Case of You', one of my favourite songs, on a stringed instrument that sat on her lap – a zither or melodeum or something. Whatever it was, it was rather beautiful.

Years later, when I was in town on tour with the Stones, I went up to see Betsy, and Joni was there as well. It was Valentine's Day in the late 1990s. I suggested that we go to Lucy's, the Mexican restaurant on Melrose that I used to take Michael to in order to cheer him up. We had a lovely meal sitting outside, because Joni was smoking up a storm at the time. Joni was driving, so after we'd finished she gave Betsy a lift back to Beverly Hills, and then took me on to the Four Seasons hotel, where I was staying. Because it was Valentine's Day, Betsy had given me a heart-shaped box of chocolates. As we pulled up to the hotel, one of my friends from the tour, a guy called Alan Dunn, watched me get out of the car and say goodbye to Joni.

'Was that who I think it was?' he asked.

I waved the box of chocolates at him. 'Well,' I said, 'it *is* Valentine's Day.'

———

I lived in old Hollywood. I had an apartment in Beechwood Canyon and then bought a house opposite. It's just below the 'Hollywood' sign – it doesn't get much more Hollywood than that!

The apartment I rented had previously been lived in by Nancy Andrews, Ringo's girlfriend. I had it painted to make it feel like mine, and it had a wonderful deck with a view of the 'Hollywood' sign. One night, I came back to the apartment, and there was a kitten sat in the middle of my parking space. It wouldn't move; it just sat there. In the end, I had to climb out of the car, scoop him up and put him to the side so that I could park. As I entered the apartment, I heard this soft padding – the kitten had followed me in. *He must be hungry*, I thought, so I looked in the fridge and found him some tuna to eat. The kitten ate it, and I thought, *There is my good deed done for the night.* I put him out.

The following morning, I opened the front door, and guess who was sat there on the doorstep? It seemed I had adopted a cat. Or rather, a cat had adopted me. I called him Bennie. God, I adored that cat. I wasn't the only one: when I popped down to the supermarket, people would say to me, 'Oh, are you Bennie's owner?' And they'd explain how he came to see them when I was out at work – he was very clever at finding other people's houses!

I used to leave the window ajar at night so that he could climb in through the space. I would hear him come through and think, *Oh, Bennie's home.* And then all of a sudden I would feel his body curled up against my back, which is where he liked to sleep. Wherever I went in the apartment, Bennie would follow. If I sat down to watch TV or went to have a bath, he'd come along, too.

When I left California, Bennie stayed with the tenant for my house. The next time I was back, I was staying with Betsy and decided to go and see him. When I got there, he was waiting outside the house. My heart melted. When I went to the car and started to head off, I could see him running after me in the rear-view mirror. I got out, scooped him up and put him in the car. I drove him back to Betsy's and said, 'You've got yourself another cat.' Betsy already had several, but Bennie just walked in and laid himself down. Usually, cats are quite territorial, but they took to Bennie right away.

'He is so natural,' Betsy said. 'One of these days he is going to open his mouth and start talking.'

Bennie liked living in Beverly Hills. Down the road from Betsy's house was Pickfair, where silent-movie star Mary Pickford lived. Bennie would go and sit on her wall. Another time, Betsy took a call asking if she was Bennie's owner. The man on the phone explained that Bennie was around at his house quite a lot, that his wife was ill with cancer and spent a lot of time in bed, and that Bennie used to go and lie down on the bed with her.

I was on tour with the Stones when Bennie died. I had been due to go and see him, and had called up Betsy's houseman, a guy called David, to arrange the visit. 'You are too late,' he explained.

He told me how Bennie had curled up on the roof of their soft-top car and gone to sleep. That was how they found him. I still miss him. If I were ever to be granted one wish, without question it would be to have Bennie back in my life.

———

In the late 1970s, I made two big changes in my life. Firstly, I moved back to New York from California. And then, having spent two years working for Rocket, I decided to move on. I loved Elton, but the atmosphere at the record label was quite political and difficult. I didn't hit it off with Robert Appere, who was head of A&R, which didn't help, and John Reid and Elton were arguing a lot. That combination of office politics and quarrelling wasn't the best atmosphere to work in. John had got engaged to Sarah Forbes, the daughter of film director Bryan Forbes and actress Nanette Newman, and there were all sorts of rows between him and Elton about that. In the end, it got so tiresome that I left.

I was sad to leave but excited by what I was about to do next. America was in thrall to a new type of music, and I was offered a job right at the epicentre: head of disco for RCA Records. Disco, for me, was a continuation of what I'd been doing in the 1960s, when Motown ruled the roost. I used to go dancing with the Beatles and the Stones at the Ad Lib, at the Scotch of St James. When I went on holiday to L'Estartit in Spain, there was a wonderful disco called St Trop, where I would turn up with a whole pile of 45s and dance into the night. I'd always loved going to clubs and dancing, so the world of disco just followed on from that.

It was in New York, 1972, where I heard those first stirrings of disco, while on my first trip to America. I had gone dancing with a girl from Allen Klein's office. She was beautiful, very striking, and she came to pick me up at the Ritz hotel, where I was staying. Security assumed that because she was Black, she was a prostitute. We were told to leave and escorted out of the building. We went uptown to this basement club in a slightly less stuffy hotel, which was where I first heard 'Outa-Space' by Billy Preston and 'Put It Where You Want It' by the Crusaders.

The following year, Elton and I went to After Dark, where we heard 'Honey Bee' by Gloria Gaynor and 'I'll Always Love My Mama' by the Intruders. Something new and different was beginning to stir, I sensed. In 1974, having sailed across the Atlantic and arrived in New York, I went to Le Jardin, an uptown, semi-posh club – a sort of early Studio 54-type scene. I heard 'Stop, I Don't Need No Sympathy' by Lyn Roman that night and knew something was going on. After that, I became hooked by the music. I was working for John Lennon in LA by now, but whenever I was back in New York, I'd go to Colony Records on Broadway and buy all the latest releases. The guy behind the counter really knew his stuff, and I never used to argue with his selections. I'd go in, ask for twenty records, take them home and play them. Occasionally, there'd be a duff one in there, but nine times out of ten they'd be brilliant.

John liked the songs I bought, too. I remember playing him 'Shame, Shame, Shame' by Shirley and Company, which he loved. I stayed at the flat John shared with May on the East Side, and he asked me to put Shirley and Company on the jukebox he had there and to fill it with other records I thought he might like. I went to Colony and bought him some early Sister Sledge – 'Love Don't You Go Through No Changes on Me' – and 'I'll Be Holding On' by Al Downing.

When I got my job with RCA, one of the first things I did was to take Vince Aletti out to lunch. Vince is a writer, critic and disco connoisseur who had been part of the scene from the beginning. Getting someone like him onside was going to be important. By 1978, disco was emerging into and taking over the mainstream, and I could see how he might be suspicious of someone like me coming in. As soon as we sat down for lunch, the first thing Vince asked me was, 'So, what are you doing in disco?' He knew my history, the different acts I'd worked with previously.

'I know it doesn't seem like it,' I said, 'but I have always been a huge fan of dance music.' I explained how I thought that disco was the Motown of the moment. We talked about some of those early disco records, such as that Intruders song, and how the starting points could be found in R&B and soul. As we talked, Vince could see that I knew my music, so he relaxed, and we went on to become bosom buddies. One of the reasons he liked talking to me was because I had a deeper knowledge of music than many others on the scene. As a result of whom I'd worked with and the time I'd spent in the industry, I had a wider knowledge of how music had changed and could see the bigger themes and trends.

There was a strong gay element to the disco scene, of course. There was a whole gang of disco promotions people; we used to call it homo-promo because so many of us were gay. The same was true with the DJs: many of those who played the clubs were gay, as were the clubs that were at the heart of the scene – places like the Paradise Garage or the Cock Ring. The Cock Ring was a great place to go: it was about 200 yards from my house, down on the corner of Christopher Street and the river. It wasn't a big club, with a very small dance floor and a hang-out bar for gay guys. We used to call it the CR Lounge, so we didn't have to say the name. The top DJs would all play there during the week, trying out their sets before the weekend. You'd go on a weekday, have a few Budweisers for ten dollars in total and enjoy a great evening dancing to one of

149

the top DJs. At the weekend, these guys would play the Flamingo, 12 West or the Ice Palace out on Fire Island.

I loved Fire Island. It's this long, thin strip of land just off Long Island. Cars and bikes aren't allowed onto it, and wild deer roam around. The houses are all wooden, with sundecks and swimming pools. I had a studio in what was called the Co-op, right opposite the harbour. Lots of other friends had apartments there, and we'd go for the weekend. I remember one time I was at Calvin Klein's house, watching him, John Reid, David Geffen and Sandy Gallin trying to get a barbecue going. It was hilarious – four gods of style, music and showbusiness, and they couldn't put a barbecue together between them. They all got in each other's way – too many cooks!

The DJ Kevin Burke used to play his famous Tea Dance on Fire Island. It was at a venue called the Botel, a yacht club, and used to run from five until seven-thirty in the evening. It was a very steamy, sexy event. Everyone wore swimwear or shorts. The venue served a drink called a Blue Whale. I can't remember what was in it, but it turned your mouth blue, so those in the know used to avoid it. You could always spot people who hadn't been there before by the colour of their mouths! The Tea Dance took place out on the deck of the yacht club, with people also squeezing into a boat parked outside and another section inside as well. There was a woman called Barbara, the heiress to a bicycle business fortune, who was always out on deck in Dolly Parton hair and make-up. Kevin would play 'Instant Replay' by Dan Hartman and 'Changin'' by Sharon Ridley to finish with – a very downtempo, sleazy number.

The disco scene was full of amazing venues like that. Another I loved was the Loft, which was David Mancuso's place. That was one of the early venues, and again, it wasn't really a club at all. It was like going to someone's house to dance, and it was in fact the loft where David lived, with everything pushed back against the walls to make a dance floor. The atmosphere there was amazing, and David would play 'Girl You Need a Change of Mind' by Eddie Kendricks, which was one of the great early disco songs.

———

The head of RCA was a guy called Bob Summer. He had taken me out to lunch to offer me the job as head of disco. He was a real classy guy, the classiest guy ever to run RCA. The two of us got on like a house on fire: he liked me and got my character, who I was.

Part of the job was to get the records out to the record pool in each city: you shipped the records out, and the people who ran the pool would distribute them to the DJs. A big friend of Vince Aletti's was Judy Weinstein, who ran the record pool in New York. She was a bit of a queen bee on the scene, a real character with a very, very dry sense of humour. I'll never forget going to her house for a party a few years later. Madonna, before she was a huge star, was there with Jellybean Benitez, whom she was dating at the time. She spilt red wine on the carpet, and I remember watching her scrubbing it for Judy, trying and failing to get the stain out.

A while later, I asked Judy if she'd ever solved the problem of the stain.

'Oh yes,' Judy said. 'I just bought another apartment.'

As part of the job, I used to go on disco tours to visit DJs in the various cities. Dance music was taking off all over, but in different ways. Chicago was where Frankie Knuckles used to play – the godfather of house. Miami was a big disco place; LA and San Francisco, too. Bobby Viteritti was one of the big DJs in California. 'Follow Me' by Amanda Lear, an amazing singer who sounds like Marlene Dietrich, was one of his big tunes. Every city's sound was slightly different.

It was great fun. I basically danced my way around America. One artist I remember taking with me was Carrie Lucas, who had a hit with a song called 'Dance with You'. Carrie was married to Dick Griffey, the founder of Solar Records, who looked after acts such as Shalamar and the Whispers. Dick wanted me to take Carrie on a tour, so I did the same with her as I'd done with Cliff Richard, except this time with a disco diva! RCA had a good roster of acts to work with, including Vicki Sue Robinson ('Turn the Beat Around') and Evelyn 'Champagne' King.

New York, though, was the heart of the scene. It had everything: the clubs, the music, the radio stations. Frankie Crocker ran New York's WBLS, a Black station that played the best tunes. I'd have that on while getting ready to go out and would never want to leave. I'd sit there, thinking, *Hurry up and play something dodgy so that I can go out.* But he never did. 'Supernatural Thing' by Ben E. King was one he always played that I loved.

The New York club scene, with its energy and happiness, was just wonderful, very joyful and hedonistic. There was happiness and exuberance on the dance floors, wherever you went. My favourite West Side disco was 12 West. The atmosphere there was always amazing. The club's back wall was lit up in purple, and people would dance in front of it holding fans and finger bells. You'd see the silhouettes of their movements and hear the ching-ching-ching of the bells against the music. I remember going there one night with Elton and Divine, dancing to a disco remix of the Four Seasons' 'December, 1963 (Oh What a Night)'. And it was.

The big DJ at 12 West was Jimmy Stuard, who sadly died in a bath-house fire in 1977. But he and the other DJs were real craftsmen. They knew how to craft an evening of disco, so that the music peaked at a certain time. They realised that a lot of the audience would be on this or that drug, so they didn't want things to peak too soon. They were always trying to time their set so that it went with the drug high.

There were a lot of drugs going round, though I never used them much myself. I was more of a drinker and smoker: a joint and a glass of champagne was the perfect combination for me. That or a gin and tonic. I've always been known for making a mean G and T: the secret is to squeeze the lemon over the ice before you put the gin in. But elsewhere in the clubs, there was a lot of speed, coke, stuff like that. There was an elephant tranquilliser people used that knocked you for six. Quaaludes as well.

The Paradise Garage was another great venue. Going there would inevitably end up as an all-nighter, and I'd get home at around nine in the morning. Often I'd go to the Pink Tea Cup, a soul-food restaurant in Greenwich Village, for breakfast. It was great: the waitresses used to argue, and when you ordered, they would respond with 'Mm-hmm'. There was another coffee shop I used to like for breakfast as well: the Silver Dollar, though that was a bit funkier and sleazier than the Pink Tea Cup.

The most famous club in that era was Studio 54. I knew the owner, Steve Rubell, quite well. Elton and I went there quite early on after it had opened. At the time, it didn't have a licence, and you had to go downstairs into the basement if you wanted a drink. Steve remembered me for arriving with Elton, and that meant I always got in. The guy on the door, Mark, was known for being difficult, but thanks to my knowing Steve, getting in was never an issue for me.

I went with Fran Lebowitz one night, Vince and my San Francisco friends on another occasion. I went with Olivia

Newton-John after the premiere of *Grease*. I wasn't present on the night that Bianca Jagger rode a white horse, but I would see her there and chat with her. I often saw Truman Capote, Andy Warhol and Roy Halston in the club, too.

I held a party in Studio 54 for Rocket Records when they signed up with RCA. It was the most fabulous do. I got all the Rocket staff to wear white and had lots of joints and poppers to pass round. Elton said beforehand that he didn't want to go, but I got him there, and once he arrived, I knew he didn't want to leave. As well as inviting celebrities, I made sure that there were characters there as well – the bicycle heiress from Fire Island, for example.

I invited loads of people from RCA Records. Those from the Black-music and the white-music departments all came together; record companies were often split in that way in the States, and I didn't want any of that separation at the party. The openness was part of what disco was about. Paradise Garage was predominantly Black, but no one batted an eyelid if you were white. I'd go there, and also to the Gallery and Buttermilk Bottoms – which my friend David Nutter liked – which were both mainly Black clubs. And Studio 54 was like that: every race, every creed, every sexual persuasion . . . whoever or whatever you were, you were welcome.

I knew that what makes a party tick is taking people from all walks of life and throwing them together. It can't just be rich folks; it has to be street people as well. The Rocket party was one that people talked about for years afterwards. Many years later, I met Ian Schrager, who was Steve Rubell's partner, at a party in the Hamptons and I mentioned I'd organised the Rocket party, and he remembered! He said it was one of the best parties that Studio 54 had ever had.

The day after the party itself, there was a board meeting at RCA. The bash had got into all the papers, and they were full of pictures from the event. Bob Summer looked through the coverage and asked what it was that had made the party such a success.

'Tony King's address book,' someone replied.

I loved all the clubs, but if I had to pick one, 12 West was my favourite. There were the fan and the finger-bell dancers, great music thumping away, everyone happy and joyful, full of that sense of being at the heart of everything. Here I was in New York, in the midst of this hippest of crowds, Greenwich Village-type people who knew where everything was at. There was nothing fake about the set-up. It was authentic and real. I can't remember the particular occasion, but I have a strong recollection of being in the middle of the dance floor there one night and thinking, *It's never going to get better than this.*

11

I'd always known that there was an anti-disco element at the time, and it was there even within RCA. Some saw it as music for gay people, and the dislike of disco was less to do with taste and more to do with homophobia and racism. I'm not singling out the record company – in a way, the attitudes there just reflected those across America as a whole. But the prejudices were not very far from the surface.

And if you didn't like disco, late-1970s America wasn't the place for you. It became ubiquitous and hugely commercial thanks to *Saturday Night Fever*, John Travolta and 'Staying Alive'. Whether you were listening to the radio or going to the cinema, you couldn't avoid it. And as with many creative movements, the bigger and more commercial it got, the further it travelled from its roots. The commercial stuff was a world away from what we were dancing to at 12 West and Paradise Garage. It was band-wagon stuff, and a lot of it was just crap. That's what killed disco in the end. When you get to a point where Ethel Merman is making a disco record, you know the moment has passed.

On 12 July 1979, at a baseball match in Comiskey Park, Chicago, DJ and disco-hater Steve Dahl encouraged fans to bring disco records with them so that he could blow them up. This was the so-called Disco Demolition Night, and to chants of 'Disco sucks!' the records were destroyed. Fans stormed the field, and the event ended in a riot. If you can find the footage online, it's quite shocking to see: unpleasant white guys doing what unpleasant white guys do.

The commercial success of disco melted away almost as quickly as it had arrived. Disco vanished, but it did live on in different forms, becoming the foundation of dance. The idea of remixing and playing around with tracks and beats continued. Styles like New Romantic had a disco feeling underneath them. So it lived on – just in different guises.

It wasn't nice, though, seeing the music you loved so publicly hated in that way. But as the 1970s became the 1980s, other things were changing, too. In politics, Ronald Reagan and Margaret Thatcher took charge in the US and the UK respectively, bringing with them a decade of more right-wing government. But for the gay community in New York, what people thought of our music or who the new president was felt secondary to what we were about to go through.

———

In the beginning, the advice was to not use poppers. People were picking up what seemed to be a particularly nasty bout of flu, and no one was sure where the pneumonia was coming from. Some suggested it might be to do with drugs. But even after people followed the advice, the pneumonia kept on coming.

Then New York gave the disease a name: GRID – Gay-Related Immune Deficiency. And then it became the shorter, more unsavoury 'gay disease'. The fact that it seemed to be virulent in the gay community specifically led to more religious elements suggesting that the disease was God's punishment for being gay.

It's difficult to describe now how horrible and dark this period was. In a way it was a bit like the early days of the Covid pandemic – no one knew what the disease was, how it would affect them or how to deal with it. But with the recent pandemic there was a sense of community in coping with the situation. With AIDS, it was more of an isolating experience: a feeling that if you were gay, you had done something wrong, had brought the disease on yourself. And rather than offering kindness and support, the wider world didn't want to know.

Some of that was down to prejudice. Some of it was fear. One of my New York friends was a beautiful man called Jamie, who'd come to New York from Brighton. His journey was fairly common: lots of gay people moved to our area of New York because of the lifestyle and the atmosphere. He got what he thought was pneumonia, which became full-blown AIDS, and he ended up in hospital. I'll never forget going to see him. He was a handsome, striking, good-looking man. But the figure I saw in hospital, I didn't recognise. Jamie had always looked after himself, prided himself in his appearance. But sat in the hospital bed, his hair was grown out and unwashed, and it hung there, long and lank. His fingernails were long, too, extending out like talons. I was cross with the nurses for letting him get into that state, but from the look on their faces I realised that they were terrified. They didn't want to go anywhere near him in case they caught the disease themselves.

In those early days of AIDS, very little was known about the disease. No one knew what was causing it or how you might catch it. And that lack of knowledge scared people. Was it to do with being gay? It was predominant in our community, but straight people were becoming unwell, too. Could you get it from having sex? From kissing? From touching? No one was really sure. And what compounded that fear and confusion were the bewildering consequences of catching the disease. Once you'd been stripped of your immune system, you were vulnerable to any sort of virus that came your way. People went blind, died of brain disease, died from all sorts of symptoms. Death wasn't easy or quick; it was a slow, painful stripping away of who you were.

One day I met another good friend, David Jackson, for lunch in Greenwich Village. He rolled up his sleeves and showed me a Kaposi's sarcoma – lesions or spots on the skin. It's a form of skin cancer, and that's what we called it; at the time we still didn't have the term 'AIDS' to describe what he was going through (Kaposi's sarcoma is a rare form of cancer that people with AIDS are particularly prone to). He ended up in hospital, too. I went to see him on one of those crisp, beautiful New York days. When I got to his room, the blinds were down.

'It's such a beautiful day,' I said. 'Don't you want to see?'

David was in a lot of pain. 'I don't want to see another day,' he replied. And so we sat there, with the blinds down, in the dark.

It was impossible to get away from the effects of the epidemic. You'd see it out on the streets. The thinness of people – not fashion thin but ghostly skeletons. Men with walking sticks being helped along by friends. People walking slowly, carefully, step by step. Those with lesions and marks. And the yellow skin, that sallow, jaundiced, haunted look. You'd catch sight of them and you'd just know.

Where once my diary was full of drinks and dates and club nights, now I caught up with friends in hospital beds rather than bars, and later at memorial services. I'd go round to their apartments to help. I had another friend, Ed Lynch, who also succumbed to AIDS. I'd go and clean his flat for him. He had a disturbance in the brain as a result of having the disease and would get short-tempered and shout at me, but I knew he didn't mean it. I used to just laugh it off, because I knew he wasn't well. Laughing was the only thing you could do sometimes, because to think about what had happened to him was simply too much to bear.

The number of friends I lost over this period, and would continue to lose in the years that followed, broke my heart then and breaks my heart still. There was a whole gang of English people who lived next door to me: Bernard, Ellis, Norman, Tony. Sweet, lovely individuals. One by one, they all died. There was a house on Fire Island, right opposite the ocean, where I'd meet up with friends and have coffee, and everyone I knew from there died, too.

Michael Harris, my beautiful friend who'd showed me California, he succumbed. I remember being in his kitchen, and him looking at me and crying. 'I don't want to die, Tony,' he said. And that broke my heart, that this big, solid, strong guy was going to die. And I knew he would: I'd seen enough people with AIDS in New York, knew the signs, knew what was going to happen. But even so, I never got inured to the pain. If somehow I'd become accustomed to it, that might have made it easier, but every time another friend became HIV-positive, it hurt just as much as the first time. I hated it when Michael got sick. Hated it. All these years on, I still miss him terribly.

These were good, brilliant men dying young. Too young. Way too young. There is a time in your life when you expect to go to funerals, but these people were dying twenty, thirty, forty years too soon. I went through that experience decades before I should have done. And I did so again and again and again. In the end, I couldn't take it any longer. I remember going to the memorial service of another friend, Kirk Jackson, and that convinced me I couldn't stay in New York any longer. I was just too tired. Exhausted.

And I was terrified, too. It was difficult to live through this time without thinking, *When is it going to be my turn?* I remember going for an AIDS test, once they had finally been developed, and being so nervous about the result. I had booked to go on a driving holiday to Vermont and took the test before I went. I got the result back – negative. I was so relieved. The receptionist at the doctor's looked at me and just said, 'You are very lucky. Most of the people that have been tested here are positive.' I felt a whole mix of emotions: lucky, yes, but also guilty that somehow I had survived when others hadn't.

As the AIDS epidemic spread, it became a political as well as a personal issue. What drugs there were to deal with it were prohibitively expensive, and there were campaigns to get the American government to bring the price down. Charities like the Gay Men's Health Crisis were set up; campaign groups such as ACT UP followed. For years, Ronald Reagan wouldn't even mention the word 'AIDS'. It was only after the death of Rock Hudson that he did, after being persuaded by Elizabeth Taylor.

In 1987, there was a march in Washington for gay and lesbian rights. Half a million people turned up. Afterwards, the AIDS memorial project was unveiled. The idea for this had come from San Franciscan activist Cleve Jones, after he learned that over a thousand San Franciscans had died of AIDS. He wanted to find a way to remember them and came up with the idea of a quilt, with each section remembering a different person who had died. The Memorial Quilt was huge: it was laid out in the National Mall and was larger than a football pitch. It was beautiful, each of the squares intricately designed. There were almost two thousand panels at this point, and over the years the quilt would have more and more names added to it. There were walkways between the different sections, so you could walk around and look at them. What I remember most about the Mall was the silence. There were so many people, and yet you could have heard a pin drop. The only sound as you walked along, trying to take it all in, was the muffled noise of people crying.

On Good Friday 1981, I woke up with the most dreadful hangover. The previous night had been a big one. I'd been to a show at Radio City Music Hall with my good friend Michele and then gone on to Better Days, a Black gay disco that I loved. It wasn't a fancy place – a bar, a dance floor, that was about it – but it had a fantastic vibe, lots of transexuals in the audience and an amazing DJ in the shape of Tee Scott. And an appropriate name, as it turned out.

The following morning – or rather, the following afternoon – I woke up with a raging headache. I felt terrible. I got up, switched on the radio and almost immediately an advert came on. 'Do you have a problem with alcohol?' The question rattled me. It was a moment when it felt as if the person on the radio was talking directly to me. Did I have a problem with alcohol? As my head thumped, I thought, *Maybe I do*. The advert continued, the voiceover reading out a telephone number. Before I could forget it, I picked up the phone and dialled. And that is how I got in touch with Alcoholics Anonymous and started down the road to getting sober.

The guy I spoke to was called Brian. We chatted, and he talked me into going to a meeting. I remember telling him I was gay. I'm not quite sure why that was relevant, but he didn't bat an eyelid – or whatever the equivalent is on the telephone – and asked me where I lived. I told him I was in Greenwich Village, and he laughed. 'You are surrounded by gay AA,' he said. 'Would you like to go to one?' I wondered if I might meet a nice, sober boyfriend and agreed to give it a go.

This wasn't the first time I'd attempted to clean up, or my first time at an AA meeting. Working in the music business, drink and drugs had always been in plentiful supply. They greased the wheels; it went with the territory. I'd never been what I'd call a heavy drinker, but all those glasses of champagne and gin and tonic still stacked up. I'd never been a heavy drug user either: cocaine was everywhere in the 1970s, but I preferred to have a joint, together with a few poppers if I was dancing. I've never liked coke that much: I didn't like the dripping sensation in the back of the throat or the overwhelming self-confidence that came with the drug – I was always mistrustful of that.

Out of drink and drugs, it was the drink that was more difficult to wean myself off. By this point, I'd been swearing that I wanted to quit booze for the best part of a decade. I've always been acutely conscious of my weight, and stopping drinking would help with that. I turned thirty while I was at Apple, and I remember saying to friends then that I wanted to be slim and sober in my thirties. But it took me another nine years, and another significant birthday, before I succeeded.

It wasn't that I didn't try in the 1970s; it wasn't that it wasn't on my mind. When Elton did those famous concerts at Dodger Stadium in 1975, I remember talking to Bob Crewe backstage. Bob was a hugely successful record producer, producing and writing all of the Four Seasons' records, and I knew him well. We used to have dinner together, and he was a wonderful, flamboyant character. Backstage at Elton's concert, I found myself noticing how well he was looking.

'You look fantastic,' I told him.

And he said, 'Yes, I am in AA.'

'Oh!' I said. I was a bit surprised by that: my image of him was as the life and soul of the party, a drink in his hand.

Then Bob said, 'And if you're as smart as I think you are, then you might want to check them out.'

I think Bob intended to be well-meaning, but his comment really stung. At the time, I thought, *Fuck you for saying that.* But somehow it still resonated in the back of my mind.

In 1978, I finally attended an AA meeting. I went with another friend, Nona Hendryx, one of the singers in Labelle, a band most famous for their huge hit 'Lady Marmalade'. I knew that Nona had managed to get herself sober, so I asked if I could go to a meeting with her. The meeting was in midtown Manhattan, and I didn't get along with it at all. All the participants went for coffee afterwards, and everyone was talking about expressing their gratitude. That really grated and got on my nerves. So I left it.

But by 1981 I felt ready. This time, I went to a meeting in the Village, which was much more my scene. I felt I was among my people, and I relaxed and got into it. I'd go to the meetings and sit there, listening to the stories. People would open up and chat, and it was incredibly powerful. Funny, too. They would really make me laugh. And after the meeting we'd go out for coffee – the 'meeting after the meeting', we called it – and carry on talking. It was like free theatre. You'd put a dollar in the hat, or however much it was in those days, and sit back and listen.

I always remember one woman, who told this amazing story about getting sober. She'd taken a limousine to rehab, drinking whisky from a glass on the way. 'Some day he'll come along,' she'd sung in the limo, 'the man I love.' When she got to rehab, she handed the glass to her driver and said, 'Toodle-oo.' And that was the last drink she had. She stayed sober, spending time down at the church helping out with the food line and doing drop-offs to those who couldn't leave the house.

I met so many amazing people there. My friend Ed Lynch was a great speaker. He got sober, but sadly died of AIDS. He wasn't the only one by any stretch: me getting sober and the AIDS epidemic happened at the same time, and several members of the group passed away. I'll never forget seeing Ed on his deathbed. He turned to me and said, 'Always remember to look up.' And that was pretty much the last thing he ever said to me.

One of the joys of AA was that you weren't judged according to who you were or what you did. I never really talked about what I did. I would refer to it lightly sometimes if I was giving a speech about sobriety, explaining that I'd been working with musicians all my life, but never went into detail. You knew and appreciated other people purely because they were getting sober. And you were just another person getting sober, and were appreciated for that. It was truly wonderful. I've been to other AA meets – when I later moved to Paris, and then back in London – and although those have been fantastically helpful, it was those early Village meetings that have always meant the most. I made friends whom I'm still in touch with now.

My sobriety was tested early on when Elton and Freddie Mercury came to town in quick succession. My friendship with Freddie is something I'll talk about properly later, but Elton and Freddie together was something of a dream ticket. They were a riot, funny and teasing and playful. They really brought the best out of each other. Anyway, I knew they were coming to New York to enjoy themselves and would no doubt be bringing a good supply of cocaine with them. So that would be a challenge! But when Freddie arrived, he didn't have any coke, so he asked me to score some for him – not the best idea, when you're only just sober. Freddie and I then went out clubbing. We went to the Anvil, and I remember being there at six in the morning, stone-cold sober, with Freddie in full flight.

'Oh, darling,' he said, 'this is just like Berlin.'

I stood there, sipping a Perrier water and thinking, *Please can I go home to bed?*

I survived that night. And I thought, *If I can survive a night with Freddie, then I can probably survive anything.*

Being sober hasn't been easy, but I've managed it and stuck with it ever since. The only time I've ever been really tempted, funnily enough, was when Elton checked himself into rehab. I was on tour with the Rolling Stones at the time, in Rome, when I received a string of messages on my phone back at the hotel. Elton told me what he was doing, and I was so pleased for him. He knew that I went to AA and was sober, but I'd never once preached or told him or anyone else what they should or shouldn't do. I've always felt my role is just to lead by example, and then it's up to other people to make decisions for themselves.

Rome is a beautiful city, and it was a beautiful evening. I was with a group of record company people sat out in a square, when I suddenly thought how nice it would be to have a glass of red wine. I was surprised by the thought: that a friend had decided to get sober, and my response was to think about having a drink. But I really wanted one because I was happy. And I resisted.

I think attitudes to drink and drugs have changed a little since then. When people drink too much, it is rather more frowned upon now. People are much more aware of the effects that alcohol can have on you. The idea of sobriety is much more accepted. Back in the early 1980s, there was something a bit shocking about going to AA. It wasn't something you talked about. But, now, I think it is much more of a given. And that's a good thing.

———

The third major change to my life in this period also started with a phone call. I'd been out at the Cock Ring and was on my way back home, when I passed a call box on the corner of the street. It was two in the morning, and the phone was ringing. I was a bit drunk at the time (this was before I got sober), so I stopped to answer it.

I was curious as to who might be ringing a call box at that time of night.

'Oh hello, Tony,' said the voice at the other end of the line. 'How are you?'

That freaked me out a bit, I can tell you, hearing my name like that.

'I am fine, thank you,' I said, after a pause. 'Though I don't think that I'm the Tony that you are looking for.'

The man laughed. 'No, you are not the Tony I am looking for, but you sound like a very nice Tony all the same.'

'That's very nice of you,' I replied, and we started to talk.

I can't remember precisely what we were talking about or why it came into my head, but suddenly I asked him, 'Are you by any chance a religious man?'

The man said, 'If by that question you mean am I a believer, then the answer would be yes, I am.'

I said, 'This might sound strange, but might you be willing to meet up and discuss that?'

'Sure,' he said. 'I'd like that.'

I took his number down and said, 'OK, we'll fix up a time to meet.' And we did.

My interest in religion, and Catholicism in particular, stretched back to when I was a teenager. I was brought up in the Church of England, and as a child I used to go Sunday school so that I could go to the boys' club and hang out and play snooker. When I got to grammar school, the Catholic boys were separated off for school prayers. I always found that intriguing.

It was probably my aunty Gladys who was the biggest influence. I found the Church of England very dry in its teachings and felt more drawn to Catholicism. Aunty Gladys converted to Catholicism in order to marry my uncle Vince. I was intrigued by that, too, and we used to talk about it. I admired her faith and the serenity and peace that it seemed to give her. Gladys said I should go and see my local priest to discuss it, which I did. But we didn't get on at all. This was when I was only just beginning to explore my sexuality, and that felt a world away from the teachings that this priest was offering. He was all hellfire and damnation when it came to homosexuality.

Despite that, I still remained curious enough to go on a pilgrimage to Rome, travelling to the Vatican and visiting all the saintly churches – the ones where you have to go up to the altar on your knees. I saw Pope John XXIII at Castel Gandolfo, his summer residence. I remember him saying, 'I bless you and all the religious objects you bring with you.' The only thing I had with me was a bag of peaches I'd bought, and I came away wondering whether they were blessed.

That conflict between Catholicism and my sexuality meant I didn't take things any further then. I had a second attempt when I lived in Lewes, following the breakdown of my relationship with Curt. I went to see a priest, who was more compassionate than the first one I'd talked to. Looking back, he was, in fact, a man who had lived an extraordinary life. During the Second World War, he had been a prisoner in a Japanese prisoner-of-war camp, where they'd broken all of his fingers. Sat across from him, I could see how gnarled and twisted they were as a result. But despite what had happened to him, the priest continued to have remarkable faith. But still I didn't cross over. My sexuality remained a hurdle that I couldn't overcome.

Fast-forward to New York, where I arranged to meet up with the mystery man on the other end of the phone. The person who turned up was a charming, bearded man called Bob McCabe. I liked him immediately. We had a very relaxed, honest dinner in the Village. We chatted about God and religion, and I spoke about the conflict between Catholicism and my being gay, and how I had always wanted to cross the line but had never quite felt able to do so. I asked him what might be a good church to go to in New York. He thought about it and said, 'Well, the best one would probably be St Joseph's, in the Village.' He explained how it was the oldest church in New York, and having heard me talk about my sexuality, suggested that I might find it comfortable there.

I went along to St Joseph's, and he was right – I liked it. I asked if we could meet up again for dinner, and this time he brought me a book. It was called *Christ Among Us*, and I still have it today. As we ate, he said, 'I've got something to tell you.' And he told me that he was a priest.

I was taken aback. 'Are you really?' I asked.

He nodded, and he told me about his parish, which was uptown. He also talked about some of his priest friends who were gay. I was really interested in that – in how they reconciled their sexuality with their faith. These priests would have dinner parties, and I got invited along. They even had a place out on Fire Island. Meeting and talking to them, I realised that there were a lot of people in the clergy who were gay and had made their peace with it. And I realised that you didn't have to exclude yourself from God's love just because of an aspect of your personality that you'd been born with. I had never made a decision to be gay; I just was. And as such, I had never understood how that could be considered a sin.

I dipped in and out of going to church. But when I got sober and started going to AA, I began to go more regularly. And at AA, I realised I recognised two of the priests. After one AA meeting, I went up to one of them and started having a conversation with him about crossing over. He told me that if I was serious, I should

170

go to the catechumenate – classes for those looking to convert to Catholicism – which took place over the winter months with someone called Sister Mary.

So that's what I did. At Easter 1982, I stood at the altar of St Joseph's church in Greenwich Village to complete my conversion, with Father Bob McCabe by my side as my sponsor. I remain in touch with him, and although he is retired, I continue to get a call from him every now and again. I still have the Bible that he gave me, which he inscribed for me, writing: 'Tony, I am delighted to be your friend, to share with you in the quest we are all making for true inner peace and happiness. May the word of Christ dwell in you in all its richness.'

Amid all the darkness of the early 1980s, I had found a ray of light that I could follow.

12

As disco went into decline, my role as head of disco at RCA became a little redundant. Instead, I sidestepped and became the company's creative director. To be honest, I never really liked the politics of the role, but I did love its creative aspects. I've always been interested in art and fashion, and I really enjoyed having the freedom to input on everything from promotions to campaigns to photoshoots to album covers.

The 1980s was very much a visual decade. In August 1981, the music channel MTV launched, famously, by playing 'Video Killed the Radio Star' by the Buggles. Beforehand, MTV came to RCA and did a presentation. I remember sitting there and thinking, *This is going to shake things up*.

Some stars got what MTV was all about quicker than others, and no one more so than Madonna. I mentioned earlier how I'd seen her at a music industry party trying to get red wine out of a carpet. The following morning, I bumped into her then boyfriend, Jellybean Benitez, and said, 'That girlfriend of yours was a bit out of it last night.'

Jellybean said, 'No, no, that is just her way. She got up at five this morning to go swimming.'

'Oh,' I said. 'She must be very ambitious.'

Jellybean gave me a look. 'You could say that,' he grinned.

Not long after, I saw Madonna at Radio City Music Hall, where she sang 'Like a Virgin' while writhing around in a wedding dress. I went with my good friend Michele Saunders, and we both thought that she was going to be huge. Madonna understood MTV from the word go and used its reach to help make her a star. Not everyone was as enamoured by it. Later, when I worked with the Rolling Stones, the record company wanted to release another single from their latest album, and Mick Jagger said to me, 'I suppose this means doing another soppy video.' But there were some great directors out there doing really interesting work – Mary Lambert, Jonas Åkerlund and Russell Mulcahy, for example.

At RCA, it was still very early days for video, and I was involved in only a couple of shoots myself. I spent more time working with artists on their style and appearance. RCA had never really used stylists before, but I brought in some great people, including my friend Michele and Patty Wilson. Greg Gorman was a photographer I used on some of the shoots. The result was a real transformation. It was truly rewarding to be able to think in that way and pull together all these different strands of style and knowledge that I'd accrued over the years. Jessica Marlow, who was head of advertising, later said I was the best creative director the company had ever had.

The role, though, wasn't to last. Working at RCA was a quite different beast to my previous jobs at Apple and Rocket. Those labels were younger and fresher and different in their set-up, driven by the music and the stars who'd founded them. RCA, by contrast, was more corporate. Everything was more complicated and political: how the marketing department related to the press department, how the A&R department worked with the creative department, and so on. At Apple and Rocket, there weren't these divisions. I liked the fact that I'd worked across the board with the different bands I'd looked after, and that structure – or rather, lack of structure – fitted in with my different skills and experiences. At RCA, it was all a bit more regimented, a bit more political. In the corporate atmosphere, rather than collaborating in the same way, everyone kept their cards a bit closer to their chests.

It was a useful part of my learning experience, being in that environment. Later, when I worked for the Stones and dealt with their record company, it really helped that I knew how that sort of set-up worked. But as useful as it was, it wasn't much fun. And it wasn't me. One of the reasons I always got on with people – John Lennon, Elton John, whoever – was because I was an honest broker. I'd tell them straight what I thought, and however much they might not have liked to hear such an opinion, they trusted me and respected my view.

At RCA, I wasn't good enough at playing the game. I could do it to a degree, but then the truth would always slip out. Sometimes I'd find myself giving an opinion, rather than just saying, 'It's fine.' Afterwards, I'd think, *Why did I have to open my big mouth?* That's who I was, and I wasn't going to change, but it meant I found myself being sidelined. I had a new boss, and he didn't take to me. I was shifted from my role as creative director and went back to dance-music promotion. It wasn't what I wanted to do, so when the opportunity to do something else came up, I took it. Fortunately for me, the opportunity was an amazing one, and it was going to shape my working life for the next twenty years.

———

In the early 1980s, the Rolling Stones were going through one of the lowest ebbs of their long and illustrious career. Relations between the band's main players, Mick Jagger and Keith Richards, had cooled to the point where they were touring without speaking to each other. Drugs were rife. Charlie Watts, I'm afraid, was taking smack, which wasn't such a great thing to be around. And creatively, too, inspiration was thin on the ground. The band's albums weren't selling as they used to: *Undercover*, released in 1983, was their first record since the late 1960s not to reach number one on either side of the Atlantic. In 1983, the group signed a new record deal with CBS, who would release the group's next four albums, together with – for the first time – a Mick Jagger solo LP.

When I heard that Mick needed help in putting his album together, I knew that this was something I wanted to do – and that I had the experience and knowledge to do it. I'd pulled together solo albums for Ringo Starr and John Lennon, so I knew exactly what to do. The fact I'd known Mick since the early 1960s didn't hurt either. Mick is a mix of many things, but one of his strongest characteristics is that he is both a gentleman and a businessman; he is kind and yet sharp at the same time.

I met up with him, and he asked me about my work and what I was doing. 'Are you happy?' he asked.

'Not really, Mick,' I replied.

We lunched, and then I waited. Eventually, Mick's lawyers got in touch to tell me I was on board, but with a proviso: Mick had stipulated a six-month trial period. Ever the businessman. But I was delighted and felt sure that I could show him what I could do.

Making the solo album was a new experience for Mick. Rather than the regular coterie of Rolling Stones people managing the process, Mick was discovering not only the freedom of striking out on his own, but also the added responsibility of having to sort everything out. When I started work on the project, everything was all over the place. I was taken back to how it had been in LA, when I'd worked on Ringo's and John's albums: it all needed pulling together. There were different producers on board – Nile Rodgers and Bill Laswell – and they were doing various mixes of the songs, which I had to sort out and get right. There was a lot of toing and froing with the record label. CBS was run by Walter Yetnikoff, who was a boss with a big reputation, but I got on well with him. In one meeting, he told me, 'My people like you because you get things done.' Having worked for RCA, and having that experience of being in the corporate world, I now knew my way around a big record company. That definitely helped.

Everything was complicated by the fact that Mick was shooting a film in Brazil at the same time. *Running Out of Luck*, directed by Julien Temple, was the story of a rock singer who goes to Rio to shoot a film and gets kidnapped. Trying to get approvals for things, I sometimes wondered if the same thing had happened in real life! I was back in London with Mick's PR, a rather grand lady called Alvenia Bridges, who was always dressed up and drenched in perfume. When she came into a room, a cloud of scent wafted in with her. To begin with, she was a bit cagey with me, as she was worried that I was going to take over her turf. Then she went off to Brazil as well, and with just me in the office, I became the one person the record company could get hold of. I went back and forth with them and Mick while shooting was going on. When we got to the stage of test pressings – the final version of the album – they flew me out to see Mick, so he could listen to them and give his approval. We made a detour to the record company's offices there, he listened, signed them off, and the album was a go.

Once the album, *She's the Boss*, was ready to be released, I switched my attention to sorting out the publicity. That all took place in Paris, where the Stones were recording their next album, *Dirty Work*. The fact that Mick was doing publicity for his solo album when he was meant to be recording an album with the band didn't help the already strained atmosphere. It was a difficult situation to navigate, and the fact I was working for Mick didn't sit well with everyone. Keith Richards, in particular, didn't like it. 'Why are you doing this?' he asked.

I was very straight with him. 'You know, Keith, it's just a job,' I told him. 'It's just a job that brings in money.' Keith was worried, I think, that I was taking sides. 'I'm not taking a dig at any of the band,' I reassured him. 'I love the band.' And I did. And I do. I was always loyal to the Stones. Whenever I spoke to Mick, even in troubled times, I would always be supportive of the group.

Keith had his own manager, Jane Rose, and to begin with she was a little guarded about my involvement. But once we started working together, we became friends. She realised that I saw the bigger picture in terms of the group. Mick might want to do his solo albums but, ultimately, he was the lead singer in the Rolling Stones. And although I was there helping Mick with his solo work, I wasn't going to do anything to get in the way of that.

———

The most successful solo hit that Mick had at the time was the cover of 'Dancing in the Street' that he did with David Bowie for Live Aid. In 1984, Bob Geldof, the lead singer of the Boomtown Rats, had been moved by reports of the famine in Ethiopia to co-write (with Midge Ure) 'Do They Know It's Christmas?' for Band Aid, a collection of many of Britain's biggest music stars of the time. This was followed on the other side of the Atlantic by USA for Africa's 'We Are the World'. In July 1985, Geldof put on Live Aid, a huge transatlantic concert held at Wembley in London and the John F. Kennedy Stadium in Philadelphia.

I didn't have much to do with the Jagger–Bowie collaboration. I remember Mick coming in one day and saying he'd just done this record and video with David, all in twenty-four hours; they did the recording first, and then shot the video at night. As soon as Mick showed me the rough cut of the video, I knew it was going to be big. The song went to number one in the UK, and I remember Mick talking about the difference it made. 'When you're number one, you go into a restaurant and everyone pays that little bit more attention to you,' he explained.

For Live Aid itself, David Bowie performed at Wembley and Mick in Philadelphia (there was briefly a plan for the two to perform the song together, but satellite delays made this impossible). The Stones weren't in any state to play as a band, but performed separately instead, with Mick doing his own solo set, while Keith and Ronnie Wood played with Bob Dylan. It was a little bit political: we knew that they were there, and they knew that we were there, but the two camps kept apart for the night and did their own thing.

The Philadelphia end of the concert was the poor relation of the two. Wembley is an iconic venue, and the production there was beautifully put together. The Philadelphia concert was much more scrappy by comparison. The John F. Kennedy Stadium didn't have the same kudos as Wembley; it was more of an open-air concrete bowl, and the concert took place in baking heat, in which the crowd roasted. While Wembley had a revolving stage for each band to get ready on, Philadelphia had a curtain, and not even a nice curtain at that: I remember looking at the stage and thinking how cheap it looked.

Charity concerts are always a bit of a strange affair. Before we flew to the States, we went round London deciding on outfits for Mick to wear. We went to Stephen Sprouse and bought a load of clothes. We went to see Nile Rodgers, who was working with the Thompson Twins at the time, and in the studio were racks of clothes for the Thompson Twins to choose from. Mick turned to me, shaking his head, and said, 'All these people are starving in Ethiopia, and we're choosing which outfits to wear.'

Mick was determined that his performance at Live Aid was going to be good. He had the focus that the top, top performers have. Being brilliant on stage doesn't come out of nowhere; it comes from hard work and attention to detail. Freddie Mercury had that drive, too, and it didn't surprise me when Queen knocked it out of the park at Wembley. When Freddie came off stage afterwards, Elton John told me that he turned to Freddie and said, 'Well, that's it. You've taken the show.' It doesn't hurt when you have the right rock anthems for the occasion, but the way Queen had woven them into that medley that night, squeezing every last second out of their allocated slot, was brilliant.

Mick was similarly prepared. He said that he would ask Tina Turner if she would sing with him, but we still needed a band. I was friendly with Tommy Mottola, and he said to me, 'Would you like Daryl and John to do it?' Hall and Oates – who wouldn't want them as their backing band? To top it off, the Temptations agreed to come on and do some backing vocals.

When Tina and Mick performed together, their medley of 'State of Shock' and then 'It's Only Rock 'n' Roll' was one of the stand-outs of the whole show. There was so much energy and electricity between them, culminating in Mick ripping Tina's skirt off towards the end of the medley. It was one of those supposedly spontaneous moments that had in reality been carefully prepared. The band had spent the previous day rehearsing, and Tina had been super-specific about what she wanted – 'Play it like this, not like that' – so that everyone was ready to go.

We were staying in a hotel near the venue, and after rehearsals were finished, Tina asked Mick to come over to rehearse some more. The pair of us went over to where she was staying. Tina wanted to practise the skirt-ripping. She wanted it done in a particular way, and she wanted it done right. It was a surreal evening. I sat there in the hotel room, watching the pair of them practising the skirt-ripping time and time again, until it was just right. Like I say, the top performers leave nothing to chance.

The effect of that practice was evident in the success of the performance. Mick went down a storm. I watched the set from out front, on the sound desk. I've never liked watching shows from the side of the stage: you don't get to see them properly. You need to be out there in the audience to really get what is going on. Whenever I can, that's always been my favourite vantage point.

The show closed with a performance of 'We Are the World' by all the artists. The organisers wanted Mick to be one of those at the front singing, which he really didn't want to do. He hid away at the back instead, and made his exit as quickly as he could.

The next day, Mick was going to LA, and he asked me if I'd like to come along. He had access to a private jet owned by MGM, this cool little plane that had a bar and all sorts of mod cons on it. I was pretty tired after all the organising I'd done for Live Aid, but I said, 'Yes, why not?'

When we got to LA, Mick said that he was going to Jack Nicholson's, and would I like to join him? I knew Jack, having met him via Betsy Asher when I lived in LA back in the 1970s, so I went. It was great to see him, but the exhaustion got on top of me: one minute I was sat on the sofa, listening to Mick and Jack talking away, the next I was fast asleep.

I woke up to see Jack staring at me in amusement. He gave me that grin of his and said, in that familiar drawl, 'Well, I'm sorry we were *so* interesting.'

The tours that Mick did to promote the solo albums – *She's the Boss* and the 1987 follow-up, *Primitive Cool* – were great fun. Away from the awkwardness of the Stones, he was relaxed and on top of his game. He had a great band behind him, including Joe Satriani and Jimmy Rip, and the fact he was having a good time rippled through the whole set-up. The entire crew and backstage team were fun to hang out with. Caroline and Isobel, who did the make-up and wardrobe, were always going off and having adventures, then coming back and filling us in on what they'd been up to. The sets themselves were a mixture of solo stuff with a few Stones songs thrown in. Mick groomed the band to sound right, and they did a creditable job on those numbers, even if it was never quite the same as the Stones themselves.

The tour went out to Australia and the Far East. In Australia, I remember Mick hiring a boat, and we all went for a wonderful boat ride around Sydney. Two incidents in Japan and Jakarta stand out. Over the years, the attitude to gigs in Japan had changed. The first time I went, I was struck by how well behaved everyone was at concerts. When the show finished, everyone would stay in their seats and wait until they were asked to leave, block by block. It was all very polite and orderly. Because of those previous experiences, we decided that when Mick played 'Gimme Shelter', he would start the song out by the soundboard, and then walk through the crowd up to the stage, and because we thought the audience would stay in their seats, it would all be fine. Something, though, had changed in the Japanese psyche since my last visit. Rather than letting him walk through unhindered, the crowd mobbed him instead, and the security guys had to wade in and push their way through to save Mick before he disappeared. The Japanese promoter came up to me and said, 'No more! No more!' He was furious with me that Mick had done that and held me responsible.

After the show, I asked Mick if he was all right.

'It was a bit hairy,' he admitted.

That show, however, was trumped by our experience in Jakarta. Indonesia at the time was ruled by an authoritarian regime under President Suharto. He'd been in power since before the Beatles split up, and the ruling junta were determined to make the most of Mick's visit. The whole atmosphere for the stay was slightly surreal. Mick was being dragged to a series of publicity events. One day, we had to go and have tea with the junta. You could immediately tell that they weren't a nice bunch of people. Then we were invited to a home for disabled people. The centre was just outside Jakarta, and we stood outside in the pouring rain. Mick was asked to get up and sing, where he was joined by a guy with no legs who danced on his hands and body. Afterwards, I said to Mick, 'I bet that was a first.' He just shrugged, smiled and said, 'No, that happened on a tour to Brazil once.'

On another day, Mick was tasked with starting a bicycle race, the Tour of Jakarta, the local equivalent of the Tour de France. After the race had begun, and the cyclists had disappeared, the crowds turned their attention to us. I was swallowed up by people and suddenly felt all these hands over my body. It didn't take me long to realise what was happening: everything I had in my pockets – money, keys, the lot – was being taken. By the day of the concert, I was ready for these strange few days to be over.

The concert itself took place at the Senayan Stadium, where they'd built a stage out of bamboo – slightly strange, but rather beautiful. The tickets weren't cheap for the locals, but it was still a huge crowd of around 70,000. I sat out at the front, as usual, next to Prince Rupert Loewenstein, who was the Rolling Stones' business adviser and financial manager. About halfway through the show, I could see that some of the crowd were turning away from the stage. I followed where they were looking and could see that behind the stadium were thick black clouds of smoke. People had been protesting about the ticket prices and were setting fire to car tyres. The crowds outside the stadium were growing ugly, and their protests were spilling over into confrontations with the military police. Or maybe the military were taking the lead. Either way, fighting and rioting were breaking out, and it seemed to be spreading into the stadium, where the crowds were breaking through the security cordons. Some people started robbing the concession stands; others were receiving the full force of the military response, and I watched as coshes rained down on the protesters.

At the other end of the stadium, the concert was continuing; the commotion was far enough away that Mick was unaware what was going on. Next to me, Rupert decided that he wasn't taking any chances. 'I'm going to go backstage,' he said, getting up.

'You're going nowhere without an escort,' I replied, fearful for his safety, and we arranged a military escort to take him back. It would have been easy to join him, but I decided to stay where I was, to keep an eye on what was going on, and also to keep Tony, the sound guy, company. It felt disloyal to leave him there by himself.

'This is not looking good,' I said to him.

But the show went on. The brutality of the military brought the rioting under control, and somehow we made it to the end of the concert. Even then, our troubles weren't over. The following day, we'd just got on the plane to leave, when it was held up. The local promoter was insisting on more money because of the riot. I'm not sure how it was our fault, but our promoter, Bill Graham, had to offer more so that the plane could take off. It was borderline blackmail, but sat out there on the runway, I think we were happy to pay to get out of there.

13

The best Rolling Stones show that I ever saw was in 1978, in Passaic, New Jersey, when they were about to start touring the *Some Girls* album. I remember going to see Charlie Watts in Woodstock, where the band were rehearsing. They played me *Some Girls*, and I thought it was just fantastic. I loved 'Miss You', which became something of an anthem during my time in New York.

Quite often before tours, the band would play some club gigs as part of the warm-up for the shows proper. And while it was amazing to see the group so close up in those venues, the problem was that they would use all the sound equipment for the tour, and everything would be too big and too loud!

At Passaic, it was the right sound system for the right venue. The Capitol Theatre was a small place, seating just a couple of thousand, and the Stones played like a small band. It was properly intimate. The group were on really good form. Mick had a new girlfriend in Jerry Hall, and everyone was relaxed and together. That came across in the performance. A few songs in, the band played 'When the Whip Comes Down'. There's a guitar break in that, and Mick, Ronnie and Keith stood together, side by side, as the solo was played. There was something about the three of them standing there that I found really powerful and moving. Later, when I worked with Mick, I always encouraged him to get closer to Keith, as I knew that every time they were together, the crowd loved it. I loved it, too. In Passaic, everything was perfect: I'd smoked a joint, the venue was great, the band were firing on all cylinders. I've seen a lot of gigs over the years, but that one remains right up there with the best.

———

By the end of the 1980s, the Stones were back together. Mick had done his solo albums, Keith had recorded one, too, and that seemed to have got something out of their system and recharged the batteries. The result was a return to form with the *Steel Wheels* album, and a huge tour in support of it. For the previous twenty years, the Stones' tours had been promoted by Bill Graham, but this time they went with Michael Cohl instead, who promised more money and a bigger cut. The tours that the Stones had done in the early 1980s had made a decent profit, but Cohl's projections took the band's earnings to another level. (The tour would go on to take $175 million, making it the most financially successful tour ever at the time.) In some respects, the model here became the prototype of how tours by big bands would work in the decades that followed. For years, tours had been there to promote the records, which was where the real money was made. But this began to turn: now the serious money was in the live performances, and the new albums were there to support that.

When I was asked to go on the tour, I must confess to being nervous. I was terrified, in fact, and thought, *I hope I'm up to it.* I'd never done a tour like this before, and not on this scale. It was one thing doing Mick's solo tours in Australia and Japan, with each leg a few weeks long, but the plan was for the Steel Wheels tour to take a whole year, going all around the world over the course of 115 concerts. Everything about it was on a huge scale. I always remember going to where the band were rehearsing in New York and being taken to see the stage for the first time. The set had been designed by Mark Fisher, and a whole load of us piled into vans to see what he'd done – the band, me, lighting designer Patrick Woodroffe and various others.

It had been set up at the Nassau Coliseum, and such was its size that it had been put in the stadium sideways, rather than at one end. Everyone was gobsmacked. It wasn't just the size of it; it was the grandness and the operatic feel, too. There were balconies, spiral staircases, catwalks, extension ramps for Mick to run along. Mark had given the set an industrial feel, with steam pipes, scaffolding and enough lights and pyrotechnics to light up a small city. It took eighty trucks to transport it. Such was its size, in fact, that it was too big for some of the venues on the European leg and had to be recreated as the smaller Urban Jungle tour there.

My role on the tour was to work with Mick in particular, act as a liaison between the record company and the different PR outfits, and manage the schedules and media requests. The number of people wanting interviews and time with the band was enormous. I had to handle that, decide who we did and didn't want to talk to, and what would work best in terms of promoting the tour. At the same time, requests from the record company would come flooding in – they wanted tickets for this concert, good seats for that stadium – so that all had to be smoothed over as well.

In the run-up to the tour, the media enquiries began to flood in. Jane Rose, Keith's manager, looked after his; I took care of Mick's and those of the rest of the band. Mick and I would sit down together and sift through what he wanted to do. The record company would send over the international demands. I always asked for separate lists for TV, radio and press to try and help manage the deluge, but that never seemed to happen. The French, in particular, sent over endless requests. Mick had a good eye here, and a good memory, too. He'd remember which magazines had a history of writing dodgy pieces and were to be avoided. It helped that he spoke fluent French; he had a chateau in France and an apartment in Paris, and he knew the French press well.

Mick was always incredibly professional in these dealings. Some musicians moan about doing press and try to get out of interviews, but Mick understood the game and what needed to be done. I remember on one occasion he did an interview for one of the big French radio stations, but something went wrong with the recording and the tape was blank. I went back to him, and as soon as he saw the look on my face, he said, 'They've wiped it, haven't they? Do you want me to do it again?' There was no hassle or complaining; he just suggested redoing it, and did it without a fuss.

Some of these interviews would be done on the road. There'd usually be a press conference to announce the different legs of the tour, and then the interviews would be squeezed in around the concerts. These would usually take place back to back on what were meant to be 'off' days, when there was no show, but often those were the days when I ended up working the hardest.

The same was true of the rehearsals. A lot of press would be done in advance of the tour, in order to generate pre-publicity and boost ticket sales. So we'd fly the journalists in, and they'd come and fit their interviews in around the rehearsal schedule. Some of the lucky ones might get to see the band playing: if the interview was going well, Mick would invite them to watch. A TV area would be arranged, consisting of three or four little sets, so that the crews could come in and set their gear out, with the band going from one set to the next to do the interviews.

If I was lucky, I'd snatch a bit of lunch down at rehearsals, but there wouldn't be much time between the interviews. And I'd have to prep the band as well. Mick was pretty clued up, but Charlie was never very interested in the press, and I'd have to explain to him who he was about to speak to, what their background was, whether I thought he'd like them, and so on.

It was by doing all of this that I got a real sense of the vast scale of the operation. Everything had to work with military precision. I also came to realise how global the set-up was. I'd wake up at six in the morning and immediately start getting faxes coming through from the UK and Europe (this was pre-digital, so it was all faxes and phone calls in those days). After a few hours, New York and the East Coast would start contacting me as well. On we'd go with the requests from California. It would be like that eighteen hours a day, for weeks, in the run-up to the tour.

———

'Continental Drift', from *Steel Wheels*, was the lead-in song of the show, and it had a bit of history to it. It featured the Moroccan music of the Master Musicians of Jajouka. Back in the 1960s, the Stones had travelled to Morocco while under threat of drugs charges in the UK. It wasn't a great trip in terms of intra-band relations, with Brian Jones's girlfriend Anita Pallenberg ending up with Keith Richards. The following year, Jones returned to Morocco, this time travelling to the village of Jajouka, where he heard the Master Musicians. This resulted in a *Brian Jones Presents . . .* album of their music being released.

Fast-forward twenty years, and it was decided to include the Master Musicians on the new album. I think it was Mick's idea, though Paul Bowles, a writer who had long been interested in the music of the area, was involved as well. The BBC filmed a documentary, *Stones in Tangier*, about the visit to Morocco. The track was recorded there, but there was a visit, too, to Jajouka, to see where the Master Musicians were originally from.

I flew with the band to Tangier. When we got there, Mick and I were taken to this grand property, almost palatial, with a beautiful enclosed courtyard. We met Paul there, and the three of us had tea together and a fascinating conversation. The next day, we met up with Bachir Attar, who was the leader of the Master Musicians, and he invited us to go to Jajouka. David Fricke, the *Rolling Stone* journalist, came along for the ride. It was quite a long drive out across the desert. At one point, we stopped at a small Moroccan town to stretch our legs. Having travelled around with Mick, I was used to people stopping on seeing him and coming up to ask for autographs, but in this small Moroccan town, no one batted an eyelid.

'You do realise no one is looking at you?' I said.

'I know,' Mick grinned. 'It's really refreshing.'

As we got closer to the village, it got more mountainous, until we could go no further by car. We did the final stretch of the journey by donkey. When we got there, it was quite a celebration. The local villagers had laid on a feast for us and also lots of *kief* – a Moroccan combination of cannabis and tobacco. I was sober, so I politely declined; everyone else, however, seemed pleasantly happy for the rest of the stay. The Master Musicians put on a performance for us – a mixture of dance and music, both with a lot of percussion. If you listen to 'Continental Drift', you can get a flavour of what that sounds like. It was a magical moment, and I was pleased when the Stones decided to use the music at the start of the concerts – a reminder of a particularly special trip.

———

The Steel Wheels tour began in Philadelphia on 31 August 1989. It didn't start well. After opening with 'Start Me Up' and 'Bitch', the sound went on the third song, 'Shattered'. Silence. Panic. The band didn't hang around, I remember that. Mick was straight off stage – it felt quite a theatrical gesture. The rest of the band followed. For five long minutes, the stage sat there, empty, looming and brooding in the dark. Out front, I could hear the murmuring and rumble of the crowd. Was everything going to be OK? But whatever the fault was, it was fixed. Mick returned to huge cheers from the crowd, and after that, the band didn't look back. The show was a triumph, and the reviews were great. The tour was up and running.

Mick and Charlie liked me to watch from out front so I could offer my opinion on how the show had gone, how it looked from out there and how the sound was. (That's why I'm deaf, by the way, courtesy of twenty years with the Rolling Stones! I have spent thousands on hearing aids over the years, I like to remind them.) I sat with the lighting guys. I got on well with them and felt part of their crew; Ethan Weber, the lighting director, even had a chair made for me with my name on the back.

I was always straight with Mick on what I thought about the show. When I worked for RCA, that candour had created dif-ficulties: here, however, the band wanted the honest truth. Any suggestions to tweak or improve things were always appreciated – the band wanted the show to be the best. On one of the tours, they played a short set on a smaller stage, away from the main one. When they walked back to the main stage, I noticed there was no music. It was dead sound, silence. Back at the hotel, I mentioned this to Mick. The following day, he brought in Peter Wolf, a good friend of his and the singer with the J. Geils Band. Together they worked up some music to play while the band were walking back. That night, it was in the show.

There were lots of changes and plenty of tinkering until every-one was happy. On another tour, the American artist Jeff Koons designed the backdrop for the stage. It had all kinds of weird stuff on it, bananas in particular. There was a pre-tour party at Norman Perry's house (Norman was one of Michael Cohl's people), and Keith jumped across a flower bed to speak to Patrick Woodroffe about it. 'That mural has to go,' he said. 'We can't have bananas up on stage. What the fuck is that all about?' When Mick got to hear about it, his response was, 'Let it go.' He knew it wasn't worth the argument. And so the backdrop was binned.

The Steel Wheels tour rolled on. Because the Stones hadn't played a tour like this for so long, there was a real hunger to see them, and a real media appetite for them as well. We got them on the cover of *Time* magazine. We had two of the biggest TV shows in America – *20/20* on ABC and *60 Minutes* on CBS – fighting to interview them. Sometimes when you're doing press, you have to really work hard to secure a slot; this time round, the media were taking me out to lunch in order to try and persuade me that I should give them the interview.

The American leg of the tour ended in Atlantic City. The show was broadcast live on TV as a pay-per-view event and included appearances from Axl Rose, Eric Clapton and John Lee Hooker. It says something about the size of the tour that Guns N' Roses were the support act at some of the shows. They were fantastic value, and there was the constant soap opera of Axl and Slash arguing on stage. One time, Axl announced to the crowd that he was going to leave the band the next day, but really it was all just part of the show. Backstage, I had a sweet conversation with him. I asked what he was doing with all the money he was making, and he said he'd bought his mum a car. He'd taken her to a showroom and said, 'Choose one.'

The Atlantic City gig was at the Convention Center, a famous venue that had hosted everything from the Beatles to Mike Tyson fights over the years. A press conference was arranged in one of the nearby hotels to announce the concert and the pay-per-view deal. The owner of the hotel was Donald Trump. Come the press conference, he was determined to get up on stage with the band. He was told quite firmly that the conference wasn't about him – it was just taking place in his hotel – but he wanted that bit of stardust and a photo opportunity with the band. The exchanges got a bit confrontational: someone started talking about trouble, to which Trump replied, 'Oh, I'm good at trouble. My speciality is trouble.' But we let him know that if he wanted to stir up trouble, we would be more than a match for him.

Trump turned up at the conference with Marla Maples, his then wife, and stood at the back, glowering, his arms folded. I was sat close to him and spent the entire time watching him. None of the press were interested in Trump; their attention was directed towards the Stones at the front. And that just seemed to aggravate him all the more. He had that Trump face of his, and I realised then what a jerk the man was. And he became president! Only in America, as they say.

When the tour reached the UK in 1990, the first of three nights at Wembley coincided with the England football team reaching the semi-final of that year's World Cup. Some people in the crowd were listening to the match on radios, and so the current score rippled out around the audience. There was a moment when England scored and a huge cheer went up. Ronnie Wood was halfway through a guitar solo at the time. Oblivious to the football, he thought they just really liked what he was playing! Later on, the band were in the middle of 'Paint It Black' when news came through that England had lost on penalties. Mick said afterwards that he could feel the audience drop. 'It was the hardest show to finish,' he said afterwards. He worked as hard as he could to get them back, despite the disappointment. Ever the pro, ever the pro.

On a later tour – I think it was Forty Licks – we arranged for the DJ and TV presenter Chris Evans to interview the band. It was great, and I remember Chris questioning Mick about what it was like to be on stage. He asked him what he did when he got out there – whether he spotted, or directed his singing to, particular people. Mick replied that he had to really concentrate and be very careful that he didn't start thinking about something at home – that his drains needed fixing, or something like that.

Having watched the interview, I asked Elton John the same question and whether he was sometimes up there singing while thinking of something else. 'Shopping lists,' he replied. 'I'll plan what I am going to do the next day, right in the middle of "Goodbye Yellow Brick Road".'

Chris also asked Mick if there was something he looked out for.

'Yes,' Mick said, 'I always look out for people who aren't enjoying the show as much. I make a beeline for them and direct my energy towards them. And invariably I will get them.' And in my experience, he invariably did.

The European leg of the tour had followed soon after the events of 1989, when parts of Eastern Europe emerged from communist rule and the Berlin Wall came down. In August 1990, after the fall of the Wall but before German reunification, the Stones played two huge gigs in Berlin, using the full Steel Wheels set. It was the first time they had played in Eastern Europe since a concert in Moscow in 1967. As you can imagine, the atmosphere for the shows was incredible – a combination of celebrating freedom and fans seeing their favourite band for the first time.

While we were there, Charlie, Shirley and I took a limo and drove out to Potsdam, just outside Berlin. All along the side of the road were sunflowers that hadn't been tended for years and were now ten, twelve feet tall. The driver told us about life under East

German rule: how those living close to the Wall could see over and watch everyone on the other side enjoying a free life; how you had to be careful no one caught you looking – any interaction with the West, and you would be reported to the Stasi.

When we got to Potsdam, the strangest thing happened. We were walking through the palace gardens there, when suddenly we heard a huge crack. We looked round and watched as this enormous tree that had died fell over right in front of our eyes.

In Berlin, I crossed from East Germany over to West Germany. At this point, the two countries were in the process of reunification, so you still had to get your passport stamped as you went from one side of the city to the other. I wanted to have that green stamp in my passport for posterity! I had a look at where the Wall was still standing: everywhere you looked, people were knocking chunks out of it. Signs of the Cold War were all over the city: in East Berlin, there were bullet holes in the sides of the buildings. Over the years, as we returned to Berlin for different tours, I watched as the city transformed. The skyline became full of cranes. The renovation of East Berlin happened at speed, and it wasn't long before the city was little different to West Berlin, similarly packed with smart hotels and restaurants.

After Germany, the tour went on to Prague. That was a huge gig, with over 100,000 people attending. The atmosphere was brilliant: with Czechoslovakia freeing itself from Russian influence, there was a real party atmosphere. The country's new president, Václav Havel, was a decent guy, young and with it. He wanted to meet the band, so a small group of us went to see him. He wanted to keep it low-key, being a man of the people, so we met in an ordinary coffee house. We were then invited to look round the presidential palace. Each of us was given a person to talk to, and for some reason, I ended up with the minister of agriculture!

14

I always knew that I wanted to find my real father. It wasn't something that I thought I could do while my parents were alive, but when they passed away, I decided that it was time to look for him. I asked my biological mother, Kay, if she minded. She gave me a look, shrugged and said, 'OK.'

'But if you do find him,' she added, 'I don't want anything to do with him.'

I didn't really know where to start looking, and I had few details to go on. I went to the Salvation Army and gave them what I knew, along with my birth certificate. I left more in hope than expectation that they might be able to find him. By the late 1980s, it was so long since he'd left that I had no idea whether he was even alive. So when I got a call back from them, I was surprised. When they told me they had found him, I felt quite churned up with emotion. They told me that I was not allowed to speak to him directly in the first instance, but that they would contact him through an intermediary to see if he was willing to speak to me.

It was his niece whom I spoke to. I explained to her who I was: 'I am Hughie Frank's son.' She spoke to him, and to my delight, he said he would be happy to speak to me.

I was working for Mick at the time and was in London. My father, it transpired, lived in Babbacombe, near Torquay in Devon. He was living in sheltered housing because he had health issues. I got on the train and headed for the West Country, not really sure what to expect. I wasn't even sure what he might look like: the only photograph I had of him was as a young dashing soldier marrying my mother. She was dressed in black, and they were stood outside a church, with soldiers around them holding their rifles up to form an arch. He was a very handsome man.

That, though, had been over forty years earlier. When I got off the train, I had the shock of my life. Instead of this handsome young man, I was met by an old guy who was incredibly frail and who made his way down the platform with a stick. I walked towards him. He looked me up and down and said, simply, 'Yes.' That was all he said. It was as though he recognised himself in me, and that was enough.

One of my skills in life had been the ability to get on with and talk to so many different types of people, but in that moment, I felt tongue-tied and embarrassed. I didn't quite know what to say. We went back to the sheltered housing where he was living, and in the afternoon, he fell asleep in his chair. I found myself taking a good look at him, trying to soak him up, because I found it awkward to look at him when he was awake. I felt odd about being there, because here he was, my real father, and I didn't sense any real father–son bond. I just sat there, feeling a bit numb. I realised, though, that when I studied his face, I could see my features. I knew, at least, that he was my father for sure.

I stayed overnight in Devon. I found a hotel, while he stayed in his sheltered housing. The following morning, I went back to see him. He got a song played on the radio for me. It was the morning show, and he rang up and asked the DJ to play 'We'll Meet Again' by Vera Lynn. I remember the DJ being a bit dismissive as he read the request out. 'Well, what did you say?' he asked. '"Where have you been all these years?"' Then he played the record, and my father sat there and cried. It was quite overwhelming, seeing him like that, thinking about time lost.

We went out, down to the cliffs overlooking the sea, where we sat in the sunshine, had a cup of tea and carried on talking. The strangest thing I learned was that he had run a pub in Pevensey Bay, down near Eastbourne. He'd lived on a street called Ringwood Road, which ran parallel to where I'd been living. He had been so close for all those years, and neither of us knew.

I asked him, 'What happened? Why didn't you come and find me?'

He replied, 'Your family wouldn't let me.'

I don't know whether that was true or not, or whether it was a good excuse for him not to bother. I never found out. It was enough just to see him. I knew who he was, and that settled something for me. I went down once more, and it turned out that that was the last time I saw him. I was away on tour with the Rolling Stones when I learned he had died. We were in Chicago. I told my friends on the show, and they were all really kind and sympathetic.

'It's OK,' I told them. 'He wasn't my dad to me, so I'm not really upset.'

My relationship with Kay, my biological mother, was difficult, too, but in a different way. In my mum's later years, Kay had moved to live round the corner from her in Eastbourne. They used to argue a bit, and my mum would ring me up in America and tell me what had been going on. I'd call Kay and tell her to stop being unkind to Mum. Kay's response was to say, 'She is impossible sometimes.'

Mum was always lovely to me. I remember once flying back on Concorde to see her, and she still said, 'Bring me some clothes to wash.' I brought her my suitcase of dirty clothes, and they were out on the line in no time, fluttering in the breeze in the back garden. The next day, they were ironed and ready to go. It was a wonderful thing for her to do for me. She was fascinated by life in

America and would ask me how much things cost, so when I told her I didn't know how much a pat of butter cost, she was shocked. So next time I visited, I made sure I knew all of the basic food prices!

In her later years, Kay had mental health problems and suffered from nervous breakdowns, and she ended up having to go into hospital. She was given electro-shock treatment and felt like a quite different person because of that. Our conversations could be fairly emotionally charged, and she could be rather unkind to me. 'You're going to end up like me,' she'd warn. 'You're going to have a break-down too.'

I think she wanted an acknowledgement from me that I was her son and she was my mother. We talked about that one time, and I told her that I couldn't bring myself to do that. 'I know that you are my birth mother,' I said, 'but I can't acknowledge you like that, because it was Mum and Dad who did all the hard work. They were the ones who put me through school and cared for me.' My loyalty was always with them.

Like my real father, Kay had her regrets. When she had a stroke and died, my brother showed me reams of notes that she had written, which he had found by her bedside. A lot of them were about me, and she'd clearly written them in an emotional state. They read as though she was obsessed with me. I was her first-born, and although she gave me away, that still had meaning for her, despite everything.

———

In 1991, following the end of the Steel Wheels tour, I went to live in Paris. I loved the city and had always had a romantic idea of it. I had visions of me sat in the Café de Flore reading the *Herald Tribune*. I'd worked in Paris for Mick when the Stones were there, and Elton had a flat there, too, which I sometimes used to go and stay in. So moving there seemed a good idea – somewhere different, a fresh start. I found an attic apartment – an atelier – with a tiny little balcony, not far from Rue Montorgueil, in the Les Halles district. That's quite a famous street now, with a market, restaurants and cafes, and is very trendy and popular, but at the time it was more up-and-coming. When I was there, they were only just laying the bricks down to make it pedestrianised.

I thought I would be happy there. As it turned out, I was exactly the opposite. Paris made me feel sad. Really sad. The beauty of the city was almost too overwhelming to bear. In the song 'I Left My Heart in San Francisco', the opening line talks about the 'loveliness of Paris' and how it was 'sadly grey'. But rather than loveliness, all I heard in the song was the *loneliness* of Paris. Parisians are not always the most sociable people, and I felt very isolated, very quickly.

One of the people who helped me settle there and find a flat was a friend called Denis. But he became unwell and was diagnosed with AIDS. It was like New York all over again. I saw him begin to fade away before my eyes. I remember him lying on the sofa, all curled up in a sort of foetal position. His mother was there, and it looked like a picture – a *Madonna and Child*. It was desperately sad.

And then there was Freddie.

———

I first met Freddie Mercury in 1976, at the Rocket offices in Los Angeles, which were on the second floor of a building in Beverly Drive, Beverly Hills. John Reid had an office down the corridor, and Queen were one of his clients. John had said to me, 'You must meet Freddie,' so when Freddie came to see him, John brought him over and parked him in my office.

We hit it off straightaway, talking for over two hours. Freddie didn't waste time, going straight into a personal conversation almost immediately. He had a girlfriend, Mary, at the time, and I asked him if he was gay.

'I think so, yes,' he replied.

'Have you told her?' I asked.

He said, 'No, I haven't.'

'I think you should,' I advised. 'It is not fair on her, and it is not fair on you, either, to go on living in a dishonest situation.'

The fact that Freddie was in the public eye also made it more probable that sooner or later it would come out, and if he didn't tell her, then Mary might find out about it in the press, which would be horrible. It seemed quite likely, too. Freddie had a lot of gay friends, and there were already rumours about his sexuality. He was hardly a shrinking violet either. Freddie heeded my advice and spoke to Mary. And that was how our friendship began.

We saw each other a lot over the years – sometimes in LA, but more often in New York. He was always a fun presence, and we would go out for dinner or to a club. He came up with this game we used to play, where you had to come up with every nondescript B-movie actress you could think of. We started that in a bar, writing down the list on a piece of paper. Lots of people used to play the game – Shirley Watts, Elton, everyone – and the list got longer and longer. There was no internet in those days, of course, so you'd scrabble around in your mind when it was your turn to come up with someone.

We'd go to different clubs in New York. Freddie loved Uncle Charlie's because it was a gay club with more of a social vibe to it. The Anvil he liked because of the sex; he went as a tourist, really – he had heard all about it and wanted to see it for himself. I'd become sober and would sip Perrier water, while he talked about how the club compared to those he knew in Berlin. He'd always call me when he was in New York. Sometimes we'd go out with people like Fran Lebowitz or Lisa Robinson. He was good friends with David Hodo from the Village People, and we'd often go out with him and his friends as well.

Freddie never used to get hassled much in the bars. Queen weren't quite as well known in the US as Elton, which helped, but also the places we were going to were pretty cool, so the clientele weren't about to come up and ask for an autograph. It was a bit like the time I took John and Yoko to Keller's, the leather bar down on the West Side. They had a pool table, with all these guys in black leather playing a game. Because they had a jukebox playing, John and Yoko were waltzing around, but no one batted an eyelid. That was the New York scene for you.

Just as Freddie would call me if he was in New York, so I would call him when I was in the UK. One night, Cliff Richard was at Freddie's house as well. We stayed up until five in the morning, and Freddie was outrageous. Cliff was very relaxed about it, and it was hilarious to watch. Freddie's arms were waving all over the place, and he was all 'darling' this, and 'darling' that, and Cliff just sat there, all sweet-natured. It was strange in a way: in terms of character they were at completely different ends of the spectrum, yet they got on incredibly well.

The best duo, however, was Freddie and Elton. To watch those two together, it was like having a front-row seat to a pair of great comedians – they would just bounce off each other. They'd talk about anything, banging on about shopping or something, and rat-a-tat-tatting off each other like two machine guns. They were

203

like the perfectly balanced double act: Freddie, all flamboyance, with his unique phraseology; Elton, deadpan and no-nonsense. (I can't remember whose idea it was, but we gave each other drag names. Sharon was Elton's name; Fred's was Melina; mine was Joy.)

I'd suspected that Freddie had AIDS for a while. I noticed that he had blemishes on his skin, and having seen enough friends become unwell, was well aware of the early warning signs. I asked him about them, but he dismissed my concerns: 'Sun spots, darling, sun spots.' But then he stopped seeing people, and that got the alarm bells ringing even louder. I remember talking to John Reid about it, and him saying, 'I think it is what you think it is.'

Every time I was in town, I would try to see Freddie. I'd call his assistant, Peter Freestone, whom we all knew as Phoebe, and ask whether Freddie was seeing people. He'd say, 'I'll let him know you're in town and see if he wants to call you.' But he never did. I was sad about that, but I respected it. I'd seen so many people go through the disease and knew they all had their own different ways of coping with it.

One day, when I was in the process of moving to Paris, I had a dream about Freddie. I dreamed that he said, 'I am glad you came to see me.' I woke up feeling quite disturbed by it, so I rang him up. This time, Peter said, 'Hold on, Fred wants to speak to you.'

Freddie came on the phone. 'How are you?' I asked.

'I'm all right,' he replied.

'I'm going to live in Paris,' I said.

'I know. Will you be able to come and see me?' he asked. 'I will send you a ticket.'

And so I went back to London to see him. It was a shock. It was about three years since I'd last seen him, and his condition had deteriorated so much. He was thin and pale. I knew he didn't have long, but we didn't discuss it. As soon as I saw him, I knew he wanted to act normally. And so that's what we did. He wanted to take me out to lunch, so out we went. He wanted to buy things. He said, 'I have seen something for your flat in Paris. It is so *Irma La Douce*,' and he bought me a table and a chest of drawers, which I still have, of course.

Freddie had got into buying art. He would go through catalogues and get people to bid for him. 'I can't believe you're doing this,' I said, when I saw the prices involved. He replied, 'Well, what else have I got to spend my money on?'

He bought a Tissot from Christie's, an absolutely stunning picture of a woman, which he had in a frame at the end of his bed.

'Look at her, darling,' he'd say to me. 'Isn't she fabulous?'

And she was.

In those strangest of circumstances – Freddie dying, me mixed up with my Parisian unhappiness – we had the most normal of conversations. We sat and watched *Oprah* together, and she had three singers on: I think it was Patti LaBelle, Dionne Warwick, Gladys Knight, performing together.

'Oh, darling, you have got to watch these divas,' he said.

Freddie was in raptures, immersed in their performance, and saying, 'How fabulous, how fabulous they are.'

The last time I saw him was at the beginning of November 1991. It was a horrendous journey. I got up at 5.30 a.m. and left for the airport at 7.30. But when I arrived, I discovered that the air traffic controllers were on strike and no planes were leaving Paris, so I went back into the city and made my way to the Gare du Nord. This was in the days before Eurostar, so I got a train to Calais, then a boat across the Channel, a train to Victoria and a cab on to Windsor, where I was going to stay with Elton. I was completely wired from all the travelling, and I'd had my bag searched by customs, too, which was upsetting. I couldn't get to sleep, but I knew

I needed to see Freddie and wasn't sure if I would have another chance to do so.

I was aware now that he was dying. He was in constant pain, and it was heartbreaking to see. I lay on the bed with him and held his hand. He was just skin and bones. And stone cold. I realised he was going to go. I spoke to the doctor and asked him, 'Are you going to make sure his last days are comfortable?' The doctor looked at me and said, 'Yes.' He knew what I meant, and I knew what he meant. I didn't want to think of Freddie dying in pain.

Freddie was the bravest man I've ever met. In all my years of dealing with friends who died of AIDS, he was the most brave. He would never let it knock his spirit. Right at the end, his spirit was still there, even as it was fading away to nothing.

———

It was all too much for me. I think, looking back, the accumulation of everything that had happened over the previous decade finally caught up with me. The death of family, the death of friends. I'd always been the person people called on when they were down or in difficulties: 'Tony will know how to handle this'; 'Tony will cheer me up.' But the weight of that responsibility began to press down heavily on me. The beauty of Paris somehow seemed to highlight all of that. I didn't really speak French either and felt increasingly lonely and isolated.

I was depressed, in a similar way to how I'd felt when I moved from London to Lewes at the end of the 1960s. I felt an over-whelming sense of sadness, a great heaviness – a sort of soul sickness, if you like. It seemed to permeate even the smallest gesture, such as making dinner or a cup of tea. I'd wake up in the morning, hoping it had gone away, and then, with a sinking feeling, realise, *Oh no, it's still there.*

It was Elton who pulled me out of it. 'You need to go to rehab,' he told me. 'You are too sad, Tony.'

And that's what I did. I got on a plane and flew to Arizona, to a centre outside Tucson. It was out in the desert, and even on the journey there, I felt different. Paris had become dark, oppressive, and was closing in on me. Suddenly, here I was in the open country, with big, sweeping blue skies and sunshine. It felt different, a change, a chance to get away from it all.

The centre was divided into different houses, with about thirty people staying in each one. Each house was named after a different type of cactus, and you shared a room. The person I shared with I'm still in touch with now. He was straight when he was there, but has since come out as gay, and is now happily married to his partner. There was a very successful American model there, too. We got on really well and used to talk a lot.

People had checked in for all kinds of reasons: alcohol, drugs, depression. A lot of people were getting sober and would go to outdoor AA meetings as part of their therapy. Those who were coming off drugs would spend several days in the hospital wing, going through withdrawal, before joining in with the group activities.

I had a wonderful therapist. Her name was Cindy, and she was lovely. I really enjoyed my sessions with her. She was very perceptive and compassionate. Some of the healing came from those meetings, and some from the group sessions. I found it really useful talking to other people. I was a good conversationalist, and because I'd had my years in AA, people who were getting sober wanted to talk to me. There was one guy there, a straight-talking Texan, who had a thing about gay people. I'd met enough people like that over the years not to be bothered by it, but despite his prejudices, I managed to win him over.

'You know what, Tony?' he told me at one meeting. 'I have tried not to like you, but I can't help it.'

I didn't cry to start with. That took a while. In fact, it wasn't until my time at the centre was almost at an end that the tears came. And then, once I started, I couldn't stop. I cried for Freddie, I cried for every person who had died, every bedside I had sat by, every memorial service I had been to, everybody I had witnessed getting sick and losing their life. It was like that book, *The Well of Loneliness* by Radclyffe Hall: I had a well that I needed to cry out.

I was in rehab for a month and continued to cry after I left. I was sad to leave. I cried on the plane back to Europe. The steward came up to me and asked if I was OK. I was, but I was a bit sad. Elton said that I shouldn't return to Paris, so I went to stay with him for a while. Then I had the chance to live in a flat owned by Seraphina Watts, Charlie's daughter, so I moved back to London. I devoted myself to painting and decorating, making the place my own. Charlie and Shirley were hugely supportive, too. I remember Shirley saying, 'Be your own man.' And I thought, *Yes, that's what I've got to do.*

I could feel myself beginning to get back into shape again. I found an AA meeting in Chelsea to go to. I was nervous and asked if I could sit by the door, in case I had the urge to leave. But I didn't. I made some new friends there and began to feel more settled. I tried antidepressants, but they didn't agree with me, so after a few days, I gave them up. As Shirley had said, I had to be my own man.

———

When I moved back to London, I was working with Rupert Loewenstein. The Rolling Stones were between tours, and I was looking for something new to do, so when the opportunity to manage Lulu came up, I was intrigued.

I'd done lots of different jobs during my time in the music business – promotions, A&R, creative director – but I had never gone into management. Working for John Lennon was perhaps the nearest I'd been to that type of role: I was a sort of de facto manager, but only on the creative side; there were other people handling the business and legal aspects. I don't think management had ever really appealed to me. It was the 24/7 aspect of the job I wasn't sure about – I like my private time too much.

Working with Lulu, however, felt like an opportunity. She was someone I'd known since the 1960s, though she admits now that I was someone she tried to avoid. She says I was a bit too much, and if she saw me at a party, she would try to keep out of my way! Lulu is a hugely talented singer, but I wasn't always certain about her choices. There was this 'bubbly' Lulu pop persona, which was a bit variety and Eurovision and Saturday-night TV, and I wasn't sure I wanted to get involved with that.

Thankfully, Lulu felt the same about her past. We met in Harvey Nichols, where she'd been shopping. She looked fantastic. Lulu has always had amazing fashion sense, but that day she seemed particularly smart and ready for business. I explained my concerns about her persona.

'If I take you on, I don't want you to do the bubbly persona.'

Lulu looked at me and said, 'Thank God, because I don't want to do that any more either. I am fed up with it.'

Lulu had always been interested in African American music, soul and blues, and wanted to be taken seriously as a singer and songwriter. She was writing a lot of stuff, which she used to play for me. One song she wrote with her brother, 'I Don't Wanna Fight', was sent to Tina Turner. It ended up on the soundtrack to her biopic, *What's Love Got to Do with It*, and was a top ten hit in both the US and the UK.

I looked at different ways to reposition her. She released an album, *Independence*, in 1993, which was a sophisticated, classy affair. I was very careful with the press, making sure she was interviewed by the right people. I got Maureen Cleave to speak to her, a great writer who had done John Lennon's infamous 'bigger than Jesus' interview back in the day. Maureen did a really good piece, as I knew she would, pointing out Lulu's sophistication and style.

We worked hard to emphasise her credibility. On *Independence*, she sang a duet with Bobby Womack. We arranged, too, for her to do a New Year TV special, where she was joined by Al Green and Eternal. And we got her out there singing. I remember taking her to be interviewed by Nicky Campbell, who at the time had an evening show on Radio 1. She did this amazing a cappella version of 'Shout', singing it all slow and ballad-like in a way that gave you goosebumps.

Around the same time, we took a call from Take That, who were fast becoming one of the biggest bands in the UK. They were planning on doing a cover of 'Relight My Fire' and wanted to know if Lulu would be on the record. I knew immediately that she had to do it. I remembered the song from my disco days: it had originally been recorded by Dan Hartman, with Loleatta Holloway doing the 'Walk on through the night' section in the middle. I knew that would work so well for Lulu: she had the right voice and range, and it would reinforce all her soul credentials. The song gave her a first UK number one.

I didn't work with Lulu for long. After three years, the Rolling Stones were about to go on tour again, and I couldn't say no to them. But I like to think I helped in repositioning her. And having avoided me when we first met back in the 1960s, she was now a true friend.

15

I worked on six Rolling Stones tours over twenty years: Steel Wheels, Voodoo Lounge, Bridges to Babylon, No Security, Licks and A Bigger Bang. A bigger bang was about right: each tour had to be announced with more commotion than the previous one, so for each press conference we tried to come up with something different in order to make it an event and up the media coverage accordingly.

For the Steel Wheels tour, we held the conference at Grand Central Station in New York, with the band arriving by train. For the launch of another tour, the band arrived on *Honey Fitz*, a beautiful boat we hired that used to belong to John F. Kennedy. On another occasion, we organised for the band to arrive by hot-air balloon, which Charlie hated because it made him feel ill. And we also arranged for the band to play outside the Juilliard Academy in New York – an outdoor performance with four songs, and another big success.

For the Bridges to Babylon tour, a pink Cadillac was hired, which the band drove over the Brooklyn Bridge to the conference. Mick was driving, if I remember rightly, with Keith sat next to him, and Ronnie and Charlie in the back. We had a helicopter filming them as they drove across, and the footage looked amazing. On the side of the Brooklyn Bridge, we put up a huge poster with the image of the lion from the album cover. I remember that as we were unfurling it, it was pouring with rain. That didn't bode well for the band's open-top car ride. But it cleared up, as New

York weather can, and by the time they arrived, it was all sunshine and heat.

There could be a bit of scepticism about these launches from others on the band's team. I remember before the Brooklyn Bridge event, Prince Rupert said to me, 'I will see you tomorrow before your *very expensive* press launch.'

I went back to find out how much we'd spent, and the cost had been half a million dollars. But in my view it was money well spent: we got the launch on the news, and ABC invited Mick and Keith to come and be interviewed. They rarely did such things together, but we made it happen, and as soon as the interview aired, tickets for the gigs began flying out of the door.

I remembered that experience when I later worked on Elton's farewell tour. I explained to everyone how you needed to have an event that would capture the imagination of both the public and the press. For Elton's launch, which took place simultaneously in London, New York and LA, everyone was given a pair of virtual reality glasses, through which they could watch the presentation. Again, the tickets went on sale straight afterwards and shifted in huge numbers.

What I also learned doing those Stones tours was that the initial press coverage was never enough. You had to keep it going, with an extra bit in the middle just to liven things up. You could never rest on your laurels. That was something I'd grasped years before, working for George Martin. I'd been plugging one of the Beatles' singles at the BBC, when I bumped into Rob Dickins, who at the time was working for a music publisher but would go on to be the chairman of Warner Music. When I told him what I was doing, he asked, 'Why are you plugging the Beatles?' He thought that because they were already established and successful, the record would sell itself.

I replied, 'The bigger you are, the harder you have to work, to show people on the other side that you are still in the game.'

It was a belief that I would continue to hold throughout my career.

———

Part of the appeal of the tours was all the different people I got to meet. It was a very social life, in terms of both hanging out with the crew and also the various individuals who turned up on the guest list. The backstage area on each tour was given a different name, but the most famous was the Voodoo Lounge, on the eponymous tour, where all sorts of the great and the good would go and have cocktails. You had to have a special pass to get in. I've still got mine in my collection.

Prince Rupert Loewenstein was great to have around, and not just for the financial and business advice he provided the band. I always loved his company: he was fascinating in that not only was he quite grand, but he also had a razor-sharp mind. He was a good listener, too, and would often act as a counsellor when things got out of hand between Mick and Keith. He'd brook no nonsense and would be quite matter-of-fact with them, pulling them back and getting them to work together again just when it seemed impossible.

Rupert would bring his various wealthy and aristocratic friends with him to the shows. I was interested in that ilk and often knew who they were – people like the Duke of Beaufort, Baron Alexis de Redé and Ahmet Ertegun. Baron Alexis was a famous boulevardier who threw the Proust Ball, an infamous party in Paris that Richard Burton and Liz Taylor went to.

I met all kinds of people on tour. One time I was collared by one of Keith's people, who said he wanted me to go to his dressing room: 'There's someone he wants you to see.' I went backstage, and there in the dressing room was Cilla Black, my old friend, who was with Tracey Emin, the artist. I adored Tracey's work and had just heard her on *Desert Island Discs*. I told her how much I loved her. We got talking about Margate, where we both had family connections, and went on to become great friends.

Sometimes politicians would turn up. One I always remember was John Major – a lovely and really interesting man, far more so than his public persona suggested. Before the gig, I asked him if he'd like a cup of tea, and he said smoothly, 'Not just now. I will let you know when I would like one.'

During the show, he was sat a few seats away from where I was sitting with the lighting crew. Halfway through, he turned to me and said, 'I think I'll have that cup of tea now.'

Later on, I stood by him as we were getting some food. He was with his wife, Norma, and he turned to her and said, 'Would you like some of this, darling?' I said to Norma, 'How nice he still calls you "darling".' She shrugged and replied, 'He's forgotten my name.'

Another person I enjoyed chatting to backstage was the actor George Clooney. When I was living in LA, there was a period when I was staying with my friend Mike Hazlewood. Next door to Mike lived an actress called Joyce Van Patten, who had a young daughter, Talia. We all used to do stuff together. We went to Big Bear Lake one weekend – Mike, me, Joyce, Talia and Joyce's boyfriend Dennis. When I moved to New York, Mike would write to me, and in one of his letters he told me that Talia, who in my mind was still twelve, had now grown up and got married to a young actor called George Clooney.

Fast-forward to some years later, and the Stones were playing in Milan, Italy. It was 2006, and the country had just won the

World Cup, so everyone was in a good mood. Among the guests at the show that night were Donatella Versace, who had come with an army of security people, and George Clooney. He was much more casual – just him and a friend. I was sitting with the lighting crew, as usual, and could see George down at the front. He was getting hassled by fans for photos and autographs, so I went down and asked if he'd like to sit with us, so that he wouldn't be disturbed.

George came up and sat with me. I said to him, 'We have a mutual friend, you know.' George gave me a look, so I said, 'Joyce Van Patten.' He looked surprised: 'You're talking about my ex-mother-in-law.' I explained how I knew her, and how she'd been Mike's neighbour. I asked him if he knew that, sadly, Mike had died a few years earlier. (I later visited the hotel where Mike died, and saw the room where he passed away.)

We had a wonderful evening, a really good gossip. I asked him what he'd done for work when he was trying to make it as an actor. I expected George to say he'd waited tables, but instead he told me he'd been a bricklayer.

'I still worry where the next job is coming from,' he said. 'As an actor, you always do.'

'It doesn't sound like you are going to be in *that* much trouble,' I said.

———

In 1999, I was in the States, on the Rolling Stones' No Security tour. We were in Fargo, when Mick decided he wanted to go bowling, so he booked six lanes in the local bowling alley, and we headed down. It was him, his kids and a small gang from his entourage. When we got there, you could see people's mouths literally drop open. I guess it's not every day you go to your local bowling alley and see Mick Jagger wander in.

It was one of those nights that made being away on tour the place to be. There's plenty of schlepping and travelling, and a lot of time spent thinking about and missing home comforts, but there are moments of camaraderie and friendship, too, and the night in the bowling alley was one of those. Everyone was relaxed and having a great time. Halfway through, Mick and I went up to the concessions stand to buy some pizza. We were talking about the pizzas, and I said, 'You know what? I think we ought to wait to eat.' I could see they were making some new ones. 'There's a fresh batch coming out in a minute. We should wait for those, rather than just buying the ones that are already here. They're looking a bit sad.'

Mick and I had this long conversation about which pizzas to buy. In the end, we decided to wait, and it was the right decision – the fresh ones were delicious.

The following day, our visit to the bowling alley was all over the news. Everything that Mick had touched, from his drinks glass to the bowling ball, was being auctioned off. And there was footage of me and Mick having our conversation about pizza, which someone had filmed and was now being broadcast on TV.

I liked Fargo. I liked the fact that it was small. I liked the fact that it was mom-and-pop stores and not shopping malls like so much of America. It was probably one of the most human places we went to, in that sense. While we were there, I remember watching a train travelling through a crisp white snowscape. I could hear the train's whistle, and I thought, *That's America*. You don't often witness that. It was one of those small but beautiful moments that stay lodged in the memory.

Memories from other tours flash through my mind. In Moscow, I remember Keith adopting a dog that had been ill-treated. One of the kitchen staff had found the poor creature. It had been kicked by the locals and was limping around. She brought it backstage, and everyone was being kind to it and looking after it. Then Keith saw it and decided to adopt it. He named it Rasputin, got it treated and took it to live with him in Connecticut. It was another example of the sweetness in Keith beneath all the bravado, which completely explains why he is so loved – by his children, his friends, everyone. It took me back to those early days, when he was in the bed in my office, talking about his trip to Chicago.

The Moscow show itself wasn't a great one. For a gig to be good, you had to get the average person in, and that depended on ticket prices and availability. The Moscow crowd was full of high rollers, and the atmosphere suffered accordingly. That wasn't the only show that was like that: I remember similar concerts in India and Shanghai, full of expats and rich people, rather than the man on the street. In contrast to Moscow, I always remember a show we did in St Petersburg, in the grounds of the Hermitage – the most beautiful setting – where the tickets were in the hands of the right people and the atmosphere was electric.

In 1998, the tour was in Germany, and I was sorting out the cover for the *No Security* live album. We wanted to get a photograph of how the stadium looked from above. A helicopter was arranged, and because I was involved, I decided to go up with the photographer. Big mistake. It was only once I was up in the air that I realised that the helicopter had half its side missing and was open to the elements so that the photographer could take his picture. We were sat there, when the pilot tipped the helicopter on its side so the photographer could get the best view. There was nothing between me and the ground below, and I was clinging on for dear life, completely petrified. When we eventually got back down, people kept on coming up to me, saying, 'Are you all right?

You look a bit white.' *So would you be*, I thought, *if you'd been through what I've just been through.*

One of my favourite memories is the Stones playing Argentina for the first time. It was always exciting going somewhere new; there was a real sense of anticipation. What would the gigs be like? How would the audience react? We got a sense of how things would go when we arrived at the airport. There was a convoy of cars and coaches for the band and crew, and as we drove out, our vehicles were suddenly surrounded by motorbikes on all sides. On the back of each one sat a second person with a camera, following our every move.

When we got to the hotel, there was a huge crowd waiting for us. Hundreds of young people were climbing and jumping on the cars. It was all a bit crazy – that out-of-control feel I remembered from those early Beatles concerts. They put up security barriers around the hotel to keep the crowds back, but even once we were inside, the madness continued, the fans staying outside all night, singing Stones songs into the night air. I was fascinated by how young they were. They were all in their twenties, yet were really digging the band.

Doing the concerts was like being dragged back thirty years in time. The shows were mad. When the band played 'Satisfaction', the whole audience had their T-shirts in the air, swinging and waving them around their heads. They loved Keith, too, and had a chant for him: '*Olé, olé, olé*, Richards!' That would ring round the stadiums – and often outside the hotels when I was trying to get to sleep at night.

I really liked Argentina and managed to see some of the country while we were there. I went with Charlie and Shirley to an Arabian stud farm because they wanted to see the horses. I got friendly with the owners and their young sons. They thought I was great because I was connected to the Stones, and they took me out to dinner, on a boat trip and to an old part of town where the tango was first developed. I watched some dance demonstrations, which were incredible. I like to think I'm not bad on the dance floor, but seeing those dancers close up, their footwork, that was something else. There were some wonderful antiques markets, too, and I loved trawling through them, finding lots of things to buy and bring home.

———

We were in Toronto when Princess Diana died in 1997. I'd been to the cinema opposite the hotel we were staying in to see *Mrs Brown*, the film about Queen Victoria with Judi Dench and Billy Connolly. When I came out, I saw Alan Dunn, who was working on the tour's logistics. He looked ashen-faced, and I asked him what the problem was.

'Diana is dead,' he said, simply.

I walked into the hotel, where there was a group of people in the lobby, including Mick, Ronnie and Ronnie's wife, Jo. We were due to go out that evening, but everyone just looked stunned. Eventually, we did venture out. Someone said that there was no point in not doing so, because we would only end up sat in our rooms alone, which would be worse. Better to stay together because of the shock of the news. It's at moments like that when you can feel a bit far away from home. Diana had always been a good friend to the gay community, and to those with AIDS in particular. I asked a friend of mine to take a bunch of flowers in my name to Kensington Palace. I wish I had seen the mountain of blooms that were left there: it must have been quite something. Instead, I was stuck in Canada. I watched the funeral with

Miranda, Mick's PA. She came to my room, and we sat in bed together, eating croissants and drinking coffee, while watching it on TV. It was very sad and very strange.

A few years later, I was back in London when 9/11 happened. I was in Soho, in a coffee bar, when someone said that a plane had flown into the World Trade Center. Having lived in New York, I knew that there were always lots of small private planes flying around, buzzing about like bees, and I assumed it was one of those. I told the guy this and got on with my coffee. Then, a few minutes later, he said, 'No, another plane has hit the other building.' It was beginning to sound a bit odd, so I got up and left. I walked along Brewer Street and noticed a pub on Windmill Street where everyone was stood outside. I pushed my way in and watched on the TV as the first building came down. The pub was rammed, but when that happened, you could hear a pin drop. I went back to the office. Mine was the only one with a TV, and all of the staff and Rupert's team were crowded round it.

'I've just seen the building come down in the pub,' I said.

Someone replied, 'The other one has now come down.'

'You're kidding,' I said. None of this made sense.

A few weeks later, I was at Ground Zero to see the site for myself. A charity concert had quickly been organised, the Concert for New York City, and Mick and Keith had been invited to take part. It was pulled together by Paul McCartney and was to be held at Madison Square Garden. Among the other acts performing were Elton, the Who, David Bowie, Eric Clapton, Bon Jovi, Jay-Z and Destiny's Child. We were given a tour of the site, which was incredibly shocking. I knew New York so well from having lived there, and to see this smouldering hole was just dreadful. We were taken around by a policeman who had been part of the rescue team, and he described how he had become choked up with soot and fumes.

At the concert, everyone was dotted about in different dressing rooms. Mick and I were ensconced in one, Elton was in another, and then there was Keith further down. It was a strange evening, seeing all these different faces I knew so well from over the years. Mick and Keith were doing two songs and had chosen well: 'Salt of the Earth', from *Beggars Banquet*, and 'Miss You'. (Elton played 'Mona Lisas and Mad Hatters', which felt similarly inspired.) 'Salt of the Earth' might not seem an obvious choice: it's a less well-known Stones song, perhaps, but it has beautiful lyrics, and the sentiment fitted the mood well.

———

It is very easy to get lost in the world of touring. Because the Stones' tour set-up was so big, you got used to travelling around the world in a bubble. I'd often go by private jet, which was always fun, though sometimes the plane would be full and they'd ask for volunteers who were willing to take a regular flight. I sometimes did, because you'd get to the hotel ahead of everyone else and have the place to yourself. It would be lovely and quiet – until the Stones' entourage arrived.

Travelling with these special people, all of them characters in their own right, made for a rarefied atmosphere. Once, I asked Charlie, who was always laid back and immaculately dressed, if I could see his wardrobe. He took me through all the clothes he had with him and some pieces from Asprey. In one suitcase, he had his collection of socks, which were all lined up according to colour. There was one pair that didn't sit quite right in his scheme, and I said so. He gave me this slightly dirty look, like I had critiqued his sock collection, but later on he came to find me and said, 'You know what you said earlier about the socks? You were right.'

It was very easy to get lonely on tour. Living in your own little world, away from your friends, you'd go to the show, with all the excitement of that, and then return to your room and the silence. The temptation was to go down to the bar, but being sober, that wasn't something I felt like doing very often. When I did, I'd get a round of applause: 'A guest appearance!' 'Her Majesty!' – comments like that. So I entertained myself in different ways. At the time of my Stones tours, internet chatrooms were the places to be. You could log in and meet people in any city, very easily. This was in the era before Grindr and other dating apps. I remember someone showing me Grindr once, and I said, 'I've been there and done that.'

I was always discreet, but over the years I met a lot of people while on tour. Brazil was always somewhere that felt particularly sexy. Staying in Rio on one Stones tour, I met a very hot young man on the beach. Young Brazilians can have a thing for older men, and he wanted to come back to my hotel. I told him I couldn't risk that, but we arranged to meet that evening anyway, on the seafront.

When I arrived, he had a beautiful white shirt on and was very handsome. 'Follow me,' he said, and he took me to a love hotel, where you could rent a room by the hour. Gay, straight – everyone was there. The room had mirrors everywhere – above the bed, on the walls. They gave you towels and lubricants and left you to get on with it.

On the same tour, we went to watch a rehearsal for the Rio carnival. The music was intoxicating, very percussive and powerful, and I got pulled up onto the dance floor by this guy. He was hot to trot and wouldn't stop dancing with me. I knew he wanted me to be his partner for the rest of the evening, but we were due to fly out early the following morning, and I got dragged back to the hotel by the others. I still regret leaving him!

The next day, when we were on the plane, someone said to me, 'I hear we had to rescue you from the dance floor.'

I just smiled and said, 'Yes, but I made up for it at the love hotel.'

Coming back from tour, it could take a while to readjust to daily life. I remember waking up at home, and there was some drilling going on in the street outside. My immediate thought was, *Oh God, Mick is going to go crazy when he hears that.* But then I realised I was at home, not in a hotel, and so didn't need to worry.

On another occasion, I remember being back home after a tour and going out with a couple of friends for dinner. They had arranged to pick me up at 8.30 p.m., and when they arrived, I stood there, waiting for them to open the car door. I was so used to the routine of leaving a hotel, a van waiting for me outside, its doors being opened, the luggage being taken from me and helped in, that I'd gone into that mode.

'We open our own doors here, Tony,' my friend said, to laughter from the others.

16

In 2005, I went to see my doctor for a medical in advance of the Rolling Stones' Bigger Bang tour. I had to go before being allowed to travel; it was something I'd done before each of the previous tours and I'd never really thought twice about it. It was just another bit of paperwork.

This time, however, things were a bit different. We were looking through all the test results, when I noticed one of them was missing.

'I can't see my HIV test here,' I said.

The doctor looked through the notes. 'You're right,' he said. 'They must have missed it off.' He buzzed his secretary and asked her to bring it in.

When the secretary came into the room, she had a look on her face. She seemed very serious and concerned as she passed the piece of paper over. I blanched. *Oh dear*, I thought. The doctor looked at the results, and I watched as his expression changed, too. He paused for a second, then looked back up at me.

'I'm afraid it looks like you have been exposed to HIV,' he said.

It was the news I had long been dreading. For twenty-five years, in fact. Was I shocked to discover I was HIV-positive? Yes. Was I surprised? No. I knew that I had been fooling around, playing around on the edges. But at the same time, I had got away with it for so long, I thought I was invincible. HIV felt as though it was something that happened to other people. But I was to learn the hard way that that was untrue. I was every bit as vulnerable and susceptible as everybody else.

The doctor started talking to me. He was trying to explain that there was medication and treatments that could deal with HIV, but I couldn't really hear a word he was saying. My mind was whirring back through the years – to Freddie, Kenny and all the other friends who'd passed away, to the disco years and New York in the early 1980s. *Am I going to be one of those people? Am I going to die?* The enormity of what I'd been told was going to take a while to properly sink in.

I had agreed to go to Tate Modern later that day with a friend, Min Cooper, the wife of the percussionist Ray Cooper. There was an exhibition by the German artist and sculptor Joseph Beuys. Beuys is quite unique as an artist, with strong social and political elements to his work. His sculptures can be extremely striking, and he uses vitrines or display cases to gather up his smaller pieces into themes. Any good art exhibition makes you think, but as I walked around, I wasn't really taking in what I was seeing. All I could hear in my head was the doctor's diagnosis and the same thought going round and round: *Am I going to die?*

Afterwards, we went for fish and chips. There's a cafe near the Old Vic where all the taxi drivers go to eat, which I always thought was a good sign. So we went there for supper, and all the time my head was spinning.

The following day, I called up one of my best friends, Andrew. Andrew is a vicar, and when I told him I needed to talk, he immediately heard the tone in my voice and came straight over to see me. As soon as I told him, I broke down completely. Through the sobs, I said that this was the worst day of my life.

'I am so frightened,' I said. 'I don't know what to do.'

Andrew is a true friend. He was kind, helpful and supportive, and he calmed me down. He asked what the doctors had said. And as we chatted, I started feeling a bit better. I remember the song

'Hey Jude' coming into my head – the line about taking a sad song and making it better. 'That's what I have got to do,' I told him, 'take a sad song and make it better.'

The good news at that point was that my CD4 number was OK. The CD4 count measures the robustness of the immune system: a healthy system will have between 500 and 1,500 CD4 cells per cubic millimetre of blood. What HIV does is to destroy these cells. The danger level is when this count drops below 200 cells/mm^3 – that's when HIV has progressed to become AIDS. The doctors checked my CD4 number and said that, for now at least, I didn't need to go on any medication. That was a relief: I was worried about being on tour and having to take a load of drugs with me. I didn't want anyone to know about my situation. In fact, the only people I told on tour were the medical team. I needed them to know in case anything should happen, in case blood was involved. They were very kind and supportive and kept the information to themselves.

Nobody else knew. I didn't tell the band, I didn't tell my friends in the crew, anyone. It was an incredibly lonely place to be. And at the same time, it was oddly familiar. I was taken back to when I was teenager and had kept my sexuality a secret. It felt like a similar sort of set-up now, except darker and deadlier. Because the tour followed on so swiftly from the diagnosis, I hadn't had time to come to terms with it before suddenly we were jetting off. I hadn't had the opportunity to talk to anyone, whether friends or therapists. As a result I had to do all that coming-to-terms stuff by myself, in empty hotel rooms around the world.

After the tour was over and I was back in the UK, my CD4 numbers started to dip. I had a chest problem, bronchiectasis, and went to see the doctor about it, and it was clear that I was now going to need medication. The main treatment for HIV is antiretroviral therapy, or ART, which works by reducing the amount of HIV (or the viral load) in the body. The treatment was developed in the mid-1990s, and I was aware of the initial side effects that the medication could give you: lumps on the back of the neck and a distended stomach, among other things. I've always been someone who has prided himself on his appearance, so this scared the life out of me.

I was lucky to have some wonderful doctors. My practitioner at St Mary's Hospital in Paddington was Nicki Mackie, whom my doctor knew. It turned out he had trained her and, he said, she was the best. I also did private therapy with a guy called Dean, who was also incredibly kind and helpful. Both of them reassured me that the drugs had been modified and the side effects I was worried about were now incredibly rare. So I started taking my medication: originally it was two pills a day, then it became one each day in the morning. As long as I remember to take it, I'm OK. Even when I get regular illnesses now, I don't worry. I have to have a health MOT twice a year, so I know that my immune system is healthy. I can get a cold, or worse, and know I can fight it off. I got pneumonia in Vegas one time, but I recovered. Recent research has shown that people with HIV are probably going to have the same lifespan as everybody else. It's a condition I've learned to live with, rather than worrying about it being one that is going to kill me.

One of the hardest things about being HIV-positive, though, is the emotional toll it takes on you. I felt shame, huge shame for having it. That was one of the reasons why I didn't tell people. I felt in some way that I'd let them down, that it was my fault, that if people knew I was HIV-positive, they'd judge me and treat me differently. I know I'm far from alone in feeling that way. In fact, it's quite common for HIV-positive people to withdraw and not tell their friends and family – at the exact point when you need the support of friends and family the most.

When I first went to St Mary's for treatment, one of the doctors said to me, 'I guess you thought you were invincible.' At the time, his comment really upset me. I thought, *Fuck you for saying that.* But it also hurt me, because it had a ring of truth to it. I didn't want to admit that, not then, but as the years went on and I reflected, I came to accept that he was right. I *did* think I was invincible. So on one of my visits to the hospital I sought the doctor out. I told him I'd been upset, but that I was OK with it now.

It might sound like a strange thing to say, but I know how incredibly lucky I've been. I think of friends who died before treatment came along in the mid-1990s, such as Freddie, and it saddens me to realise that if the drugs had arrived a couple of years earlier, they would probably have been OK. That dividing line between HIV as a death sentence and a condition that allows you to still live a normal life is brutal. It feels so arbitrary that they lost their lives, while I'm still here. It's hard not to feel survivor's guilt sometimes.

You worry about the stigma attached to being HIV-positive, but some of that, I've learned, is self-inflicted. Society has changed: we're in a different, more tolerant world than the UK and US of the early 1980s. People are a lot more accepting of it now, and that's been helped by those HIV-positive people who have been open and honest in talking publicly about their experiences. When I was first diagnosed, I envied their ability to do that. It was something I was incapable of.

To begin with, the number of people I told was tiny. I didn't even mention it to really good friends for years. I remember telling Elton. He was in King Edward VII's Hospital with an illness, and I went to visit him. I hadn't planned to tell him, but we were sitting

231

there talking, and he turned to me and said, 'There is something different about you these days, Tony. You are a lot calmer and softer. It's like you have changed into somebody else.'

And I just told him. 'I'll tell you why that is,' I said. 'It's because I'm HIV-positive.'

Even having told a few people, I still kept my condition mainly to myself. Writing about it in this book means that lots of people I know will be finding out about it for the first time. I did wrestle with whether to mention my condition at all, but I think it's important that I do. And if I can sit here and write, 'I am HIV-positive,' then I hope that might encourage others in a similar situation to come forward as well, knowing that it is OK.

———

I was on holiday with Elton in St Tropez, when he asked me what I was doing with the Stones. They weren't on tour at the time, but I was still being paid a small retainer as part of the staff.

'They're not really giving you very much to do over there, are they?' he said.

He was right. I explained that they were between tours and also that the people involved were changing. Prince Rupert Loewenstein had gone, and it sometimes felt as though there were more lawyers involved now. It did have the feel of something gradually coming to an end.

'I'd like to give you something to do,' Elton said. 'But I don't have anything in mind right now.'

A year later, we were on a boat again, going to St Tropez for lunch. On the way home, he said to me, 'I haven't forgotten what I said to you a year ago, you know.'

A year or so later, I am in my flat, when he rings me up.

'It's Elton,' he said. 'I have got a bit of a surprise for you.'

'Do I stand or sit?' I asked.

And he said, 'Your choice.'

I stayed standing. 'So, what is it?' I asked.

'I need a creative director for my Las Vegas show,' Elton said, 'and I was wondering if you would be interested in it.'

Now I had never done a show, never art-directed and videoed an entire event, but my instincts kicked right in. I knew exactly what was required, so I said yes. What I didn't know when Elton asked me was how little was already in place: he didn't have a stage, he didn't have a creative director, he had only a few months to go before the show was meant to open and he was virtually in tears. And that was the point at which he called me!

We spoke again that evening, and I asked, 'So, what does this mean?'

'It means that you will be getting more money than you are with the Rolling Stones,' he replied.

We started talking about the show, and he asked me what I thought of Mark Fisher and Patrick Woodroffe. I said, 'I have worked with them for the last twenty years with the Stones, and they are the best.'

'OK,' said Elton. 'Then we'll get them.'

Mark and Patrick agreed to be involved. They recommended a guy called Sam Pattinson, who had done a lot of visuals for the Stones and U2. He was to prove integral to the success of the show as well. Sam and I immediately started working together. We had another meeting with Elton, and I went through the suggested setlist with him. He wanted to start the show with 'Rocket Man', which I didn't think was right. Everyone else was nervous about changing the running order, but I was quite happy to tell Elton what I thought.

'This is Vegas,' I said. 'You've got to start with "The Bitch Is Back".'

And so we shifted that to the beginning. I moved a few other songs around as well – 'Philadelphia Freedom' I remember putting further back. Elton's response to all this was, 'Do what you have to do.' He gave me carte blanche to shape the show as I saw fit.

Sam and I got to work on the visuals, pulling together the videos that would be playing behind Elton while he played the songs. The piece for 'Goodbye Yellow Brick Road' was animated and based on Alan Aldridge's drawings for *Captain Fantastic*. It was a very beautiful film that went through Elton's career. For 'Mona Lisas and Mad Hatters', we involved Jennie Livingston, who had made a wonderful film called *Paris Is Burning*. I explained to her that Elton is a great photo collector, and that what I wanted to do was show a series of semi-stills of New Yorkers throughout the song. The pictures would not be completely frozen; instead, the individuals would turn their heads or do something else. Again, it was a stunning film.

As we were doing the pieces, I said to Sam that we had to make sure they weren't too difficult to understand, that they must connect emotionally. Elton's market in general, and the Las Vegas market particularly, is what could be described as Middle American. We had to give the crowd something not too convoluted that was enjoyable to watch. My ambition was that when people left the show, they liked Elton even more than when they had come in.

Jo Hambro and I styled the show together. We styled the clothes and the colours, then worked with Richard James, from Savile Row, on making beautiful suits in deep plum colours. I had this idea of drawing on what I called 'Renaissance colours' – those rich reds and greens that you see in paintings of the Tudors. We had Swarovski crystals stuck onto the suits, which came with its own

234

complications. The clothes needed to be flown to Swarovski in America, and their people asked for the temperature of the plane they would be flown back in: if it was too cold, they told me, the crystals would fall off. So I had to find a way to store them in a special part of the plane, and thankfully they arrived back OK.

When Elton got to Vegas, we showed him what we'd been working on, and he was delighted. We had filmed a tribute to Elizabeth Taylor to play in the background to 'Blue Eyes', and Elton cried the first time he saw it. I'd found a picture of Liz in her pomp, around the *Suddenly, Last Summer* period, and she looked gorgeous.

The stage itself was amazing. Mark and Patrick had done an incredible job. It was elegant and beautiful, and had all these nice little touches, such as pictures of Elton's dogs, carved into the design. Once we started to rehearse, I would make notes and change things around. I got the sense that some people weren't used to that. They'd look at me as if to say, 'You've got some nerve.'

But that was my job, creative director, and I wanted the show to be just right. During 'Mona Lisas and Mad Hatters', for example, Elton had all the backing singers grouped around the piano. It didn't look great, because if you looked under the instrument all you could see were their legs. I said to Elton, 'We do not need the backing singers up there. All we need is you at the piano, the guitarist and one of the cellists. We will light it simply and beautifully, and it will look fabulous.' Elton agreed, and we redid it. Everyone admitted that it worked much better.

After the rehearsal, Elton asked me if I was happy with everything. 'Not totally,' I said.

I still wasn't happy with the 'Tiny Dancer' footage, but I was more worried about 'Don't Let the Sun Go Down on Me'. The song really needed to grab the audience's attention. I said to Sam,

'You are going to find out that this is when the temperature goes up about ten degrees. You do that song, and then you are into the home run of hits – "Crocodile Rock", "Saturday Night" and so on.'

Sam, thankfully, wasn't fazed by this at all. He had a very low-key approach to everything, so he said he'd take a look.

The next morning, I came in and saw one of the guys working on a visual on his computer, with all these beams of refracted light. It looked beautiful, and I was delighted when he said it might be for 'Don't Let the Sun Go Down on Me'. I worked with Sam to get the timing right: there is a moment in the song when the key changes, and the visuals had to respond in intensity accordingly. It looked great. And when Elton dedicated the song to me during the set, it meant that much more.

The show went on to become the most successful residency in Las Vegas for years. The only reason we stopped doing it was because of the planned subsequent tour, otherwise we could have gone on selling out. I was so proud of it. In fact, I have never been so proud of anything as that. It was a massive feather in my cap, and I was pleased Elton had asked me to do it.

———

When Elton decided to do his final tour, Farewell Yellow Brick Road, Sam and I worked together again, this time alongside David Furnish. We took the Las Vegas element of the original show and took it on the road, turning it into a much bigger, more rock-and-roll version. David came up with lots of really good suggestions and ideas, and the three of us pulled it off.

I was particularly proud of some of the new pieces. For 'Philadelphia Freedom', we auditioned a load of dancers from New York, put them in outfits in striking colours and let them strut their stuff. It was simple but hugely effective. We got Martin Parr to take photographs for 'I Guess That's Why They Call It the Blues'. He's a marvellous photographer and took amazing pictures of people at the seaside, old pensioners in deckchairs, that sort of thing. We held a competition in which people were asked to make videos for three Elton songs that hadn't had one on original release: 'Rocket Man', 'Benny and the Jets' and 'Tiny Dancer'. We showed them at the Cannes Film Festival, and we ended up using the 'Tiny Dancer' one.

I was as proud of the Farewell tour as I was of the Vegas show. The only shame was that the run was overtaken by events and the tour was put on hold because of the Covid pandemic. We were barely halfway through. But the show must go on, as the saying goes, with the tour scheduled to be completed in 2023.

———

In between Vegas and the Farewell tour, I worked with Elton on all sorts of projects. By this point, there were two parts to Rocket: Rocket Entertainment and Rocket Management Company. The management company looked after all sorts of different people, including the singer Anne-Marie, Rag'n'Bone Man, Alexandra Burke, one of the winners of the TV show *X Factor*, and in his early days, Ed Sheeran.

Ed was often around the office back then. He's a lovely guy, modest and sweet. And he loves cats. We always got on really well. Sometimes I'd come in and find him asleep on the couch in the office – exactly like I used to find Keith Richards all those years before.

I remember being called in by Elton to a meeting, when Ed was about to launch his second album, *X*. He'd recorded an amazing song called 'Sing', which featured Pharrell Williams. Elton played it to me, and I said immediately, 'That's a smash.'

Elton said, 'Yes, but Ed wants to put it out as the second single.'

I turned to Ed and said, 'Don't do it.' I explained how long I'd been in the business and how I'd seen people make this mistake so many times: that they had this great song but were going to save it for the second single. 'What happens is that the first single doesn't do the business, and as a result the second single, which sounded like a massive hit before, now sounds like less of a massive hit and struggles.'

Elton and I persuaded him, and the single became his first number one.

There were some great albums that Elton wrote during this period, and I did my bit to help on them in any way I could. One I particularly loved was *The Diving Board*. Elton wanted to go back to writing something straight and simple: piano, bass and drums. He brought in some great musicians to work with and T Bone Burnett to produce it.

After it was recorded, I was asked to listen to a playback of the album with Elton and T Bone. When it finished, they both looked at me for my opinion.

'It sounds great,' I said. And it did. Simple, sparse and beautiful. 'But it's way too long. You need to cut it down.'

They both looked horrified at that: they were clearly very proud of the album.

'Which one would you chop?' Elton asked. So I told him. Later on, he said to me, 'That's why I like working with you. Because you always give me good advice.'

Around the same time, Elton was given the Brits Icon award and invited to do a show. This was a new venture for the Brits: a separate concert for the artist who'd won the Icon award. The concert was shown on ITV and featured music from Elton, inter-spersed with video messages from various stars, including Ringo, Yoko, Ed Sheeran and Billie Jean King, among others. As you can imagine, I was heavily involved in putting that together, arrang-ing for the different artists to talk about their memories of Elton. Later, I spoke to Carol, half of the Carol and Shirley double act who used to work at Apple.

'When I watched that, I thought, *This is so classy,*' she told me. 'I said, "I bet Tony is involved. His fingerprints are all over it."'

As the Covid pandemic took hold in 2020 and the Farewell tour slid to a halt, I worked on one last Elton project. *Jewel Box* was a sort of extended companion piece to his *Diamonds* greatest hits collection. This, however, was a selection of deep cuts from throughout Elton's career. It was a monster box set: nine CDs of music, including B-sides and previously unreleased early tracks. If you're an Elton fan, it's an absolute treasure trove . . . or jewel box!

Box sets are one of the directions that the record industry has gone down in recent years – high-spec, high-end products for the discerning fan. Elton asked me to help with the design and the packaging. The set came with a lavish, hundred-page book. I had the idea of doing it in collage format, based on a Cecil Beaton book that I had. There was plenty of material from throughout Elton's career to use, and so we got to work on it.

It's the kind of project I really like. Over the years, I've visited so many places, been to so many galleries, have accumulated all this knowledge of art and photography and style and fashion. And whether it is a Vegas show or a lavish box set, I'm able to draw on these influences and pull it all together.

In a way, my own life has been something of a jewel box. Looking back over the different memories I have from sixty years in the music business, I've been lucky to see and work with so many of the greatest stars in rock and roll. If you'd told that young boy in the kitchen in Eastbourne hearing Elvis Presley for the first time how his life was going to turn out, he would never have believed you. But to borrow from that song, I found a new place to dwell that day. It might only be rock and roll, as another song has it, but I've liked it ever since. I wouldn't have lived my life any other way.

EPILOGUE

In August 2021, I had a particularly shocking few days. On Friday the 20th, I was diagnosed with Parkinson's disease. On the Sunday, I took a phone call from Barry, the husband of my goddaughter Seraphina, to say that her father, Charlie Watts, was terminally ill and didn't have long to live. And on the Tuesday he died.

To say I was broken-hearted at his loss is an understatement. I adored the man. Over the years, I'd spent so much time in his company, a friendship that had grown ever since I'd helped look after his unwell cat in the mid-1960s. We were family: I was godfather to his daughter and granddaughter. I worked on the Stones' tours for twenty years, and it was always the two of us who would hang out. We'd laughed and messed about together around the globe.

Covid meant I hadn't seen Charlie for a while. The last time I'd seen him, appropriately enough, was on Savile Row. Appropriate, of course, because of how sharply dressed Charlie always was (back in 1969, before the infamous Stones concert in Hyde Park, I remember him coming round to my flat in Fulham to iron his trousers!). I'd met him by chance. He'd come up behind me to say hello, giving me the surprise of my life. I had a bag with me that he'd bought for me once as a gift, and we'd chatted away as normal, saying goodbye as though it was an everyday thing. I had no idea that would be the last time I'd see him.

A few weeks later, Seraphina invited me over for dinner. Again, I hadn't seen her for a long time. It was a beautiful evening, and we reminisced about her father. Seraphina said that she and Charlotte, Charlie's granddaughter, wanted to set up some sort of celebration of his life, and I said that would be a wonderful idea – to remember the good times that he'd had over the years.

In early December 2021, the memorial event took place at Ronnie Scott's in Soho. Thanks to Covid, everyone had to take a PCR test before going, but once inside that historic venue, it was like being transported back in time. There were so many familiar faces: Charlie's relatives and the Stones' 'family' of friends and crew, too, people I'd been on tour with but hadn't seen for years.

It was a wonderful evening of memories and music. Jools Holland hosted the event. He did a boogie-woogie piece with Dave Green, one of Charlie's oldest friends, whom he'd known ever since they'd grown up together. Tim Ries, the Stones' saxophonist, played a tune called 'Blues for Charlie', which he'd composed specially for the evening. Lisa Fischer and Bernard Fowler, both long-time Stones vocalists, sang 'Trouble in Mind' and 'Up Above My Head'.

Then it was time for the Stones. Mick, Keith and Ronnie ambled their way up to the stage. Seeing them up there took me all the way back to another tiny venue in Soho, to which I'd first been dragged by Chrissie Shrimpton. It was strange to think that gig was half a lifetime ago. Back then, the audience had been nonplussed and indifferent. Now, the atmosphere was filled with warmth. The band played two blues numbers: 'Shame, Shame, Shame' and 'Down the Road Apiece', a Chuck Berry song they recorded on one of their early records.

I spoke to the Stones. I was touched by how kind they all were. Keith was pleased to see me, and Mick and I chatted away just like back in the old days. The fact that we hadn't seen each other for years just melted away. Friendships, like great music, have that timeless quality.

I told Mick about the fact that I had been diagnosed with Parkinson's. He gave me a look, then there was that trademark shoulder shrug and smile.

'Oh well,' he said, 'I guess that just means we'll have to have a slow dance.'

ACKNOWLEDGEMENTS

I would like to thank everyone who has been involved in the making of this book. In particular, I would like to thank Robert Caskie, Anita Land, Alexa von Hirschberg, Hannah Knowles, Hannah Marshall, Mo Hafeez, Joanna Harwood, Mike Jones, Ian Bahrami, Dan Papps, Catherine Daly, Sam Pattinson, Stella Scott, May Pang, Sam Emerson, Claude Gaussian and Sam Taylor Johnson. Finally, many thanks to Tom Bromley for turning my eventful life into a story.

IMAGE CREDITS

Page One
With Mum, Aunty Gladys and Dad at the seaside. Courtesy of
the author.
St Andrew's Junior School picture, aged eight or nine. Courtesy
of the author.

Page Two
With my brother Peter and biological mother, Kay, Eastbourne
seafront. Courtesy of the author.
In the back garden in Eastbourne, with Chico the family dog.
Courtesy of the author.

Page Three
With Peter and Kay, Eastbourne seafront. Courtesy of the author.
With Mum and Dad in the back garden, 1961. Courtesy of the
author.

Page Four
Aged fifteen. Courtesy of the author.

Page Five
In L'Estartit, Spain, 1966. Courtesy of the author.
With my biological father, Hughie, late 1980s. Courtesy of the
author.

Page Six
With Neil Sedaka. From the author's collection.
With Brenda Lee, mid-1960s. From the author's collection.

Page Seven
With the Ronettes, Phil Spector, George Harrison and Tony
Hall, 1964. From the author's collection.
With Roy Orbison, mid-1960s. From the author's collection.

Page Eight
With Ketty Lester, my first plugging success. From the author's
collection.
With Pattie Harrison, on the way to the 'All You Need Is Love'
recording, June 1967. Courtesy of the author.

PLATE SECTION TWO
Page One
With Elton, 1973. Courtesy of Sam Emerson, shared with
permission.

Page Two
Dressing up in a photo booth with John Lennon, Lexington
Avenue, 1975. Courtesy of the author.

Page Three
With John in Calico, on our way back from Las Vegas, 1973.
Courtesy of May Pang, shared with permission.

Page Four
Backstage at Madison Square Garden with John and Ray Cooper,

1974. Courtesy of Sam Emerson, shared with permission.
With John and Elton, on our way to Boston, 1974. Courtesy of
Sam Emerson, shared with permission.

Page Five
Rehearsals for the Madison Square Garden show, 1974. Courtesy
of Sam Emerson, shared with permission.
The *Mind Games* advert shoot, with John, 1973. Courtesy of
May Pang, shared with permission.

Page Six
With Freddie, 1981. Courtesy of the author.

Page Seven
With Mick Jagger, 1987. From the author's collection.

Page Eight
Backstage with Keith Richards and Ronnie Wood. From the
author's collection.
With Charlie Watts, 1995. Courtesy of Claude Gassian, shared
with permission.

INDEX

253